Invisible
Hand

Invisible
Hand

Overcoming Obstacles and Challenges

Karren Y. Alexander

Christian Living Books, Inc.
An Imprint of Pneuma Life Publishing
Largo, MD

Christian Living Books, Inc.
An imprint of Pneuma Life Publishing, Inc.
P. O. Box 7584
Largo, MD 20792
301-218-9092
ChristianLivingBooks.com
info@christianlivingbooks.com

ISBN   1-56229-210-2
ISBN13   978-1-56229-210-2

Printed in the United States of America

Cover design
by Michael D. Jackson (MasteryofMarketing.com)

Dedication

To my mom, Flonetta, and in memory of my dad, Willie Alfred. Thanks for teaching me that there's no such thing as can't. I love you.

Acknowledgments

First giving honor to God; Your Word is indeed real in my life and sustains me. Many times I sought You for strength and guidance. I'll continue to stand on Your Word, which encourages me to "look unto the hills from whence cometh my help, for my help comes from You the maker of heaven and earth" (Psalm 121:1-2). God I sought You for help and You delivered.

Michael, my husband and friend, I love you. Thanks for your prayers and support and for being a jovial, calming force in my life.

William Royce, Alfreda, Reginald, and Ken, thanks for your love, prayers, and words of encouragement.

Sean, Quincy, and Crystal, I love you guys.

Table of Contents

Introduction

"Do you have phantom hands?" he asked. *Phantom hands*, I thought. I'd never heard of phantom hands. I frantically started searching through the files in my mind to recall and hopefully respond intelligently. However, nothing came back. It seemed as if minutes had passed, even though it was only a few seconds. *Well*, I thought. *I'll just have to expose myself and let him know that I have no idea what he's talking about.* I looked at him with a big smile and said, "What are phantom hands?"

Prior to the amputation of my hands, my mom said I was a busy child, independent and inquisitive. When we arrived home from the hospital, I walked around at home and then it happened. That child before the accident was back. The busy one, the independent one, the one who talked, walked, smiled, and played.

Right then and there at the age of three I knew that I was a winner, that I had a "can do" spirit and decided to refuse to give up. Death knocked at my door while I was lying in bed at the hospital, but the grace and mercy of God said no. I didn't have hands anymore, but life should be cherished and enjoyed, and there was much in store for me.

I learned early in life that self-acceptance coupled with a healthy attitude was the foundational principle to endure and persevere in life's journey. The Bible tells us that what a person thinks in his heart is who he becomes (Proverbs 23:7). In other words, you become what you think. It's not what others think about you; it's what you say about yourself that matters. It's what you say about yourself that becomes the truth. If you think you're unworthy, you'll never feel good about yourself. Therefore, you are what you believe.

So many people ask me, "How do you do that?" Often they follow up with, "How can you live like that?" I've learned that these questions mean different things to different people. What people are really asking me is "How do you accept yourself? How do you persevere in life? How do you obtain confidence, courage, and determination to live?" Many people end the conversation by saying, "I wouldn't be able to do it."

My life thus far, like anyone else's, has had its share of challenges and obstacles. But for the most part it's been an exciting journey of self-discovery, self-love, and self-acceptance. I've embraced God's Word, which states that I'm carefully and wonderfully made. Thus, for me, the making of my physical attributes didn't begin and end in my mom's womb but continued until the age of three. The meticulous and adorable design was finally crafted and ready to blossom into the adult I am today.

This book provides the keys for success—the keys I use to strive onward despite the obstacles and see challenges as opportunities and accept myself for who I am and what I have. Success is generally defined as the favorable or prosperous conclusion of endeavors or the gaining of wealth, position, or the like. However, I'd like to extend this definition to include being satisfied, happy, and full of joy. Thus, the definition for "total success" is the accomplishment of your goals and dreams with a fullness of joy.

We've either seen or heard of people who are successful materially but are not happy. There are people who claim happiness or joy who really could be if they fulfilled their dreams. What is certain is that no one can be successful by sitting back and not trying. Also, I've decided that a person can't be totally successful without the true source of our help, the Lord God Almighty.

First Corinthians 15:10 states, "But by the grace of God I am what I am." Well, I am what I am, I have what I have, and I can do all things that I'm empowered to do. I've learned that I'm responsible for grasping the empowering authority for me. I know that I have supporters and cheerleaders in each corner, but most of all I've learned to become my best supporter. We are empowered to manage our attitudes and emotions. That authority was not delegated to someone else to manage for us; it's ours to manage.

The keys I use are powerful and have enabled me to live a successful life. I've learned that it's the *doing* that encourages or motivates me to continue.

But be doers of the word, and not hearers only, deceiving yourselves. For if anyone is a hearer of the word and not a doer, he is like a man observing his natural face in a mirror; for he observes himself, goes away, and immediately forgets what kind of man he was. But he who looks into the perfect law of liberty and continues in it, and is not a forgetful hearer but a doer of the work, this one will be blessed in what he does. (James 1:22-25)

In being *doers* we can actively pursue joy, peace, and love. We're able to be strong and courageous and have faith in God.

I'll also describe how God has enabled me to strive to achieve total success through His love, grace, and mercy. I believe and trust Him, knowing that I can do all things through Him for He is the source. Therefore, I don't have the option to not believe and trust in His Word. I must at least try to do things, and when I do, it's just simply amazing—from driving to sewing to whatever it may be for that moment, for that snapshot of time in my life.

Psalm 31:14-15 and Romans 8:28 respectively state, "But as for me, I trust in You, O Lord...My times are in Your hand.... And we know that all things work together for good to those who love God, to those who are the called according to His purpose." This scripture speaks to the faith I have in God to ensure that I fulfill His purpose here on earth. Thus, I must know without a doubt that His hand isn't shortened and that it's there to assist me. His hand is there to ensure that I'm successful in accomplishing the task set before me. Although I can't see His hand, I can feel it as it assists me to accomplish so many things.

A few doctors have asked, "Do you have *phantom hands*? Do you have the sensation of actually having fingers?" The answer is yes because the nerves are not damaged in my arms; however, what I feel is far beyond what they ask.

What I feel is the hand of God touching me, physically and mentally, His hand providing the help I need to do everything I can do, such as driving. His hand helping me accomplish the things that some people take for granted, such as writing.

I hear His voice when He speaks to me, as He gives me alternate ways to accomplish a task or complete a project. God, the Master Creator, imparts the power of creativity, which often has me in awe.

Adults always ask me, "What happened to your hands?" However, children always ask, "Where are your hands?" It's interesting that children ask *where* as opposed to *what*. For the children I always respond, "God has them," which generally puts them at peace, especially those who know of God.

I was at choir rehearsal one evening at my former church. A little girl about five years old was sitting in the soprano section with her mother. She spotted me from afar when we were rehearsing a song and ran as fast as she could toward me. I hoped she was coming to say something to one of the other ladies in the alto section, but she was focused on me. When she finally arrived she asked loudly, "Where are your hands?" I quietly responded, "God has them." She looked at me and turned to walk away. But then she stopped, turned around, and said, "Do you want me to go get them for you?" Of course no one had ever asked me that question. But I looked at her and said, "No, thank you. I'll just wait until I get to heaven."

In the pages to follow, I'll share some of my challenges and obstacles, my ups and downs, my highs and lows. Most of all I'll share how my experiences, coupled with the keys for success, help me to persevere. The keys for success are in empowering words such as *motivation, courage, positive attitude, determination,* and *faith.*

I've accomplished many things in life thus far. My most successful and amazing accomplishment is the ability to drive a car without any attachments or devices. In this book, I use the driving techniques and operating care of a car to illustrate how the keys for successful living can be used.

Most importantly, I decided that I had to embrace me, love me, and accept me to achieve a progressive and successful life and career. I knew I wanted to become a person who lived beyond satisfaction and achieved the impossible. I wanted to demonstrate to people that despite what it may look like, and regardless of what people may say, I can do it.

Living beyond satisfaction to a life full of joy is not only my desire but should be everyone's, including yours. You can become what you think. Do you think of yourself as successful? Then you can become successful! Desire it, require it, and obtain it – the freedom to rise above the challenges to live a life full of joy.

Let's unlock the shackles and let our negative experiences become a springboard to a fulfilling life. Let the invisible hand of God, the unseen yet gentle force, embrace you. Let it direct your actions and lead you through the obstacles and challenges of life. Enjoy the walk through memory lane, embrace the empowering keys discussed in each chapter, and be prepared to use the keys in a new and different way to propel you to a more exciting and fulfilling journey in life.

Chapter 1

Your experience is less significant than how you feel on the inside after the experience.

Chapter 1

The Early Days

Look at Me

$\mathscr{I}$ was driving west on Interstate 10 in New Orleans toward the downtown area listening to a wonderful gospel song and singing at the top of my lungs. It was a beautiful yet hot and humid summer day, about ninety degrees. The skies were clear with no clouds in sight for miles away. I couldn't believe my supervisor approved my leave request. We were working on a major project that sometimes required me to work ten or twelve hours a day, and yet my supervisor told me I could take the day off. It was great to be off!

I was going downtown to attend a church conference at the Superdome. I finally arrived and hurried inside to pick up my registration package. While I was standing in line, I realized I was not the only one excited about the conference. When I walked into the dome, I was amazed at the thousands of people in attendance. I was amid a crowd of worshippers from neighboring churches, other cities, and countries from around the world.

The band started playing music, and the choir led us in a series of beautiful praise and worship songs. People all over the Superdome were singing and moving from side to side, clapping their hands and stomping their feet keeping beat with the music. Sometimes we moved fast, other times we moved slow. It was an awesome atmosphere.

When I was growing up my dad and mom played the organ and piano at church, and by default we sang in the church choir. I grew up with music in the home and lots of singing. I always loved to hear my dad sing because he would be so happy playing the piano.

For me music is a means of ushering in peace, tranquility, and an abundance of joy. So I was in my zone singing along with the choir and the thousands of people. I knew some of the songs they were singing because we sang them at church. But then we began to sing this song I had never heard before. I listened attentively to capture the words because I had already caught on to the melody.

The people around me were entranced as they sang what seemed to be the same lyrics over and over. What were they singing? The music was beautiful but I didn't quite understand the words. I continued to listen to the people around me and finally understood what they were singing with such passion and fervor. I couldn't believe what I was hearing!

As soon as I realized what I had started to sing, I stopped. Everyone was singing the words "Look at me." Look at me? What a beautiful song, but I wasn't going to sing that song. Why would I want to sing a song telling people to *look at me*? That was ridiculous.

I really wanted this song to end; however, it seemed as if they sang the song for an hour. I was standing there wondering if people were actually going to look at me. I motioned with my mouth as if I was singing the song, but fear gripped my spirit. I just couldn't do it—couldn't say those words.

Whew! The song was finally over. What a relief. Hopefully, I made it through that part of the service without people *looking at me.*

Time to Wash

February 3, 1964, was a beautiful and bright sunshiny day in Alexandria, Louisiana, a city often referred to by locals as CenLA, which means central Louisiana. My parents were a young couple with four small children. During those days they had a wringer washing machine, which was many steps above cleaning your clothes on a washboard.

This machine was around for several years and automated the process of removing dirt and soil from the clothes. However, those washing machines didn't have an automated spin cycle to extract the water out of the clothes. The water was extracted by feeding the clothes through the wringer positioned at the top of the machine.

After my mom fed the clothes through the wringer to extract the water, she would hang them on the line to dry. I'm sure I had watched this process for days, weeks, and even months. In my mind I had mastered the clothes-washing cycle: wash, wring, hang.

It didn't take long to accumulate several loads of clothes in our home. Therefore, my mom would wash several times during the week. This particular day was great for washing clothes. The smell of clean cotton blowing in the wind on a sunshiny day is refreshing. I lay in bed pretending to be asleep as I watched my mom. *That machine is amazing,* I thought.

"Flo, the phone!" Aunt Vert yelled. My mom stopped what she was doing and rushed next door. It was my grandmother calling from Shreveport, Louisiana. *Great,* I thought. *I can help wash clothes and see how this machine works.* The most fascinating part of the wash cycle was to see the clothes coming out of the wringer. They came out on the other side flat, pressed together, and ready to hang on the clothesline. Simply amazing! *I must give it a try.*

As soon as she went out the door, I jumped out of bed and scurried to the kitchen. I pushed a chair next to the washing machine, stood on the chair, and watched the clothes moving around and around. The machine stopped. *Great,* I thought. I leaned over to grab a few pieces of clothing out of the washing machine. I started putting the clothes in the wringer when suddenly my fingers got caught in the wringer. As the wringer rolled inward, my fingers and then my hands were pulled through. I tried to pull them out but I wasn't strong enough. The safety switch didn't go off on the machine because my arms were too small to signal a problem. I was barely conscious as I stood there wondering what was happening.

My mom returned home and couldn't believe her eyes. She almost went into shock because what she saw couldn't be happening. She was only gone a few minutes. There I was standing on the tips of my toes in the chair with my right side tilted toward the machine. My hands were stuck between the wringers of the washing machine. My right arm was being pulled in more and more as the wringer rolled over my arms. "Oh my God!" she screamed as she ran toward me and shut off the machine.

The rolling action of the wringer burned my blood vessels, and the doctors couldn't get the blood to flow. After freezing my arms for seven days in an attempt to save them, the doctors told my parents that my arms would have to be amputated below the elbow. They feared that if they waited any longer gangrene would set in, and they wanted to save as much of my arms as possible.

After two surgeries and twenty-three days in the hospital, my parents brought me home. They watched as I looked around and explored my surroundings. I missed being at home. I missed my toys and my siblings. I missed being free to run around and play. However, I knew that things had changed.

It took a while to learn how to keep my balance when I walked. Many people don't realize that your arms help balance your body. Maintaining my balance was sometimes a challenge.

However, I quickly relearned how to hold things, such as a bottle, ball, and fork. Yes, I was told that at three years old they would often find me sucking my baby brother's bottle. Yet, to their amazement, I was quickly learning to adjust.

Many people tried to tell my parents that I'd be disabled for the rest of my life. They said I wouldn't be able to do the things other kids would do. A doctor told my mom that I'd never be the woman I could have been if I had hands. Many people, of course, thought they were helping.

What they didn't know was that God was on my side. They didn't know that there was a plan and purpose for my life which included the amputation. They didn't understand that what the devil planned as the worst situation that could ever occur was the best because God was in control.

My parents didn't understand why it happened. Why did their little girl lose her hands? Was it a test of their faith? What had they done wrong? They didn't have any answers. Many people blamed my mom and dad. Others blamed the doctors.

Were the doctors experienced? Did they consult with other physicians to ensure they did everything to save my hands? Many people had a need to blame someone for the loss of my hands. They had to blame someone for this tragic accident. Those folks never understood that the loss of my hands was preordained and part of my destiny.

My parents didn't understand in all their hurt and pain that the God they served, the God they talked and sang about day after day and week after week, was still on the throne directing and orchestrating His master plan. They were so sad. Despite their own guilt, they had to deal with ridicule and criticism from other people.

In the midst of not understanding why I lost my hands, my mom understood that she had to continue to pray. She knew that she couldn't lose hope and deny God. She had to trust Him with all her heart, her soul, and her mind. Despite what happened she had to give Him praise.

My dad's favorite pastime was playing the piano and singing. Oh, how he loved to sing. He'd sing this song: "I'll let nothing separate me from the love of God, I'll let nothing keep me from trusting in His Word. If I turn away from Jesus, tell me where should I go? For my trials and tribulations, there's no other help I know. I'll let nothing separate me from the love of God." I wonder if in the midst of his pain, he believed the words of this song.

Children's Hospital

When I was eight years old, the doctors in Alexandria recommended that my parents take me to a hospital in New Orleans so I could get fitted for prostheses. At that time the hospital was called the Crippled Children's Hospital. What a horrible name for a hospital. All the children there had some type of disability.

It's so cold in here, I thought as we sat in the waiting area of my first visit. The temperature must have been about forty degrees, or at least it felt like it. My mom put her arms around me to keep me warm.

I looked around and saw a lot of children in the waiting room. All of them had hands so I didn't see anyone like me. Most of them were in wheelchairs or walking with crutches. I noticed that several of them didn't have legs. I watched as people went in and out of the *big room*. This was the room where the doctors and hundreds of other people (so it seemed) dressed in white sat to exam you.

"Karren Young," I heard the nurse say. My heart began to palpitate as my mom and I walked toward the voice in the other room. Before going to the big room you had to visit the nurse. This part of the exam wasn't fun. "Open wide and say ah," she said. I gagged as she placed the tongue depressor in my mouth. The last part of the nurse's exam was tough. *No!* I wanted to scream. *I don't want to take my shoe off.* Since I didn't have hands, they had to draw a sample of blood from my big toe.

We waited a few hours to see the doctor before they finally called my name. The doctors reviewed my case and referred me to Lambert's to be fitted for my first set of prostheses. I stayed at Children's Hospital in New Orleans for almost eight months to learn how to use the prostheses.

The Prostheses

By the age of eight I had learned how to eat, how to put on my clothes, how to write, and how to do a lot of other things they were trying to teach me to do with the prostheses. The prostheses were brown with metal hooks on the end. The hooks were designed to replace my hands and give me the capability to open and close things as well as grab or pick up items.

It was frustrating at times trying to use the prostheses because I didn't understand why I needed them. What was wrong with the way I'd been doing things? The doctors didn't understand that I didn't need the prostheses. I was adjusting fine without them.

The physical therapist at the hospital eventually taught me how to use the prostheses, which was an interesting experience especially during mealtime. I had to learn how to open my milk carton, but a lot of times I would waste the milk because I squeezed the carton to hard. Early on I went to my room hungry every night because the food would fall off the fork and back onto my plate or on the floor. I became discouraged just trying to eat and would give up.

Their solution was to feed me. As an independent child, however, my solution was: "Let me take these things off and eat." But that wasn't an option, so I chose hunger and waited for the eight o'clock in the evening peanut butter and jelly sandwich.

I had a lot of friends at the hospital. My best friend was a girl who didn't have hands or legs. After being at Children's Hospital for eight months, I was bored and ready to go home. I missed being at home and running around outside. We rarely went outside to play at the hospital. This wasn't normal for me because my neighborhood at home was full of kids running and playing outside.

Well, I'm ready to go home, I thought. I'll never forget calling home. My mom answered the phone. "Mama, the doctor says I can come home!" I said. By that weekend I was back at home.

School Days

I attended the public schools, and to many folks' amazement I was good academically. For whatever reason some people think that all physical disabilities equate to a mental disability. I wore the prostheses when I went to school, but I didn't wear them at home.

The prostheses were awkward and required more work than I had the time and patience for. I noticed the other kids were more creative with name calling when I wore the prostheses versus when I didn't. Thus, I needed to figure out how to get rid of those things!

One day I had a grand idea. I was talking to my mom and said, "Mama, can I wear my prostheses on top of my school dress instead of under my clothes?" After hesitating a minute or two, she said yes.

We had these large, thick bushes in front of our home aligning the sidewalk. The bushes were very full in the spring and summer and stood about three feet tall. They were so beautifully aligned that they provided privacy between our home and the streets. I looked at the bushes every morning as they grew with the seasons.

As the bushes became fuller and taller, I knew that my plan would work. The bushes would serve as my drop-off spot. *Oh, this is going to be great*, I thought. Who would tell? Who would say anything?

The day arrived. I would execute the plan the next morning. That night I went over my plan to ensure that my timing was right and I wasn't missing anything. Every night we had to say our prayers. I quickly recited the traditional Lord's Prayer; however, later that night I prayed, "God, please don't let them find out. Please don't let me get in trouble."

That morning we got up as usual and dressed for school. My mom gave us a final once-over before we headed out the door. I purposely lingered behind just a little bit. I had to be sure I was the last one to get a goodbye kiss. This was the day of new beginnings.

When my sister and brothers walked out the door, I watched them to make sure they were preoccupied with the other kids in our neighborhood. I looked to the left and then to the right and quickly took off the prostheses and threw them in the bushes. I moved so fast I almost fell down. I saw that they were sticking out from under the bushes so I folded them and stuck them under the leafy branches so no one could see them. I ran as fast as I could to join my siblings and neighborhood friends.

We had to walk about five blocks to get to school, and by the fourth block I noticed that no one had said anything. Wow, no one noticed that I didn't have the artificial arms.

11

The kids in our immediate neighborhood were used to seeing me without the prostheses so they actually didn't notice that I wasn't wearing them. So far, so good. The real test would be at school. The teachers hadn't noticed that when I did my class assignments I would take my arms out of the socket of my prostheses to complete the assignment and then put my arms back into the sockets. We had one more block to go, and then we would have to walk around the corner to go through the school gates. The principal was standing at the gates greeting the students. I squeezed into the middle of our little group. With my head held down, I quickly walked through the gates with the group of kids so he wouldn't notice. *Great! No problem.* Now came the challenge of making it to my classroom.

At the end of the day I was pleased with myself. No one had teased me all day. A lot of people looked at me but couldn't figure out what was different. I felt good. The day was a little stressful because I didn't know how the teachers would react, but the plan was almost complete.

After school I had to get ahead of my sister, brothers, and the neighborhood kids to put on my prostheses before I got home. Eventually my sister and brothers helped me. It was fun having a little secret. I kept this up for weeks. This was absolutely great. I kept telling myself that I was free. It felt so good.

Eventually, my parents found out about the secret, but much to my surprise they agreed that I didn't have to wear the prostheses anymore. Every year prior to that my mom took me to New Orleans to see the doctor and get refitted for prostheses. When we went to New Orleans for one of my appointments, my mom told the doctors I didn't need the prostheses anymore. She said, "Please use the money to pay for another child's prostheses." Although the doctors didn't agree, they respected my mom's decision.

I was glad when the trips to New Orleans were cut from a couple of visits per year to no visits. The last time I saw the doctor was when he signed my consent form stating that I could take a driver's education class.

The Past Cannot Be Changed

There's generally an event, situation, or experience that causes us to significantly alter our course or plans in life and develop a cycle of imposed limitations. These alterations or limitations can cause us to abandon our dreams and goals and render us powerless. Our creative thinking is stifled. Unfortunately, many people begin to think and feel less about themselves.

Imagine you're water flowing freely in a stream. In the stream are rocks and brush which are there to steer you as you flow along on your journey. Generally your flow is easy and free of obstacles, but there are some high and low points.

The high points are the times when you're flowing close to the surface of the stream, which propels you forward at a fast pace. This is when you're accomplishing your goals and not experiencing any significant obstacles along the way. The lows are times when you're flowing closer to the materials in the bed of the stream, which slows your pace. During these times you've hit a few obstacles and had to take the time to study, meditate, and learn from the wrong turns you made. Despite the highs and lows, you're able to accelerate and decelerate as needed and continue moving forward.

All of a sudden there is a sound of rushing wind as a large oak tree falls in the stream with a loud splash. Leaves and branches fly everywhere, startling you and hindering your ability to move forward. The splash finally settles and you see that your path is blocked by the tree. You're trapped and can't continue. What do you do?

For as he thinks in his heart, so is he.

(Proverbs 23:7)

At this moment, what are you thinking? Do you try to flow down the stream? Do you believe that your journey is over because you're faced with a challenge? Do you give up because you think you're not smart enough to determine an alternate course? Are you thinking, *This idea was ridiculous. How did I ever think that this journey would be successful?* Do you dislike yourself because of what has occurred or what you're going through?

Oftentimes we feel defeated when a challenge presents itself. We lose hope and don't want to continue. The hurt, pain, or disappointment is too great. Just like the tree suddenly falling into the water, our lives can have an unexpected crash or fall. Something unexpected falls in our path and temporarily hinders our progress. However, it's during these times that you must remain confident. You must have a strong belief in your ability to recover and regroup.

You must think you're victorious and know that you can succeed. You must know that you have the right to a life full of joy despite the challenges that are presented and know that you are more than a conqueror. Most of all, you must know that you can't give up!

Don't you know that immediately after an event occurs it becomes the past? The past is defined as any time previous to the present time. It is in the present that we begin to think about what occurred. We can think about what occurred in terms of ensuring that it doesn't happen again, but we can't change the past. That is, the past is past.

Eventually your thoughts should propel you into action, empowering you to overcome the challenge. Your mind embraces and reconnects with truth. And as you reconnect you begin to have a renewed sense of power to succeed.

You are the water attempting to flow down the stream, and now your journey has been delayed. The tree falling in the stream represents a significant event that temporarily hinders your life's journey. The length of the delay is in your control. Your next steps should demonstrate your ability to reassess your situation and eventually continue onward.

You have choices and decisions to make. Can you flow in a different direction? Of course you can! You can map a new route or forge onward and maneuver through, around, or over the challenge.

Why do people keep the past alive in the present? Is it because they don't want to accept who they are? Are they afraid? Many people dwell in the past because it's easier to give up than to keep trying.

Prior to the dreadful event, many people understand their course in life. Their life map was based on dreams with defined courses. They knew what to expect and were aware of challenges they could face. However, because of this dreadful event they fear the unknown. What else lies around the corner if they insist on pursuing this particular course or try something different? Look at what happened! They don't want to go on. They decide to stay right there.

What would you do? Whatever you do, don't stand still; don't give up. Identify alternatives. Set a new course. Don't let this event cause you to become stagnant, which could lead to sluggish, dull, and negative thoughts.

We're in control of managing how we move forward despite what occurred. Also, we're in control of assuring that we don't mentally place ourselves in jail by confining ourselves to the same place where and when the event occurred.

A jail in the physical sense represents a place of confinement. You have many limitations. You're limited to a certain area with defined dimensions. Because of your past events, you're limited to what you can do, when you can go, where you can go, and how you can get there. You don't have any control over your life for a period of time based on the offense.

This is true for a mental jail as well. A mental jail causes you to place extreme limitations on yourself. You're unable to succeed because you've chosen to dwell on the past. Depending on the event, your confidence, drive, attitude, and motivation to persevere have diminished.

You've limited your ability to succeed. You're not in control of what, when, where, and how to persevere. You can't do what you need to do, when you need to do it, where you need to do it, and how you will do it.

You dwell on the event over and over in your mind, meditating on it day and night. Your thoughts are held captive and you feel there's no way out, but 2 Corinthians 10:5 states, "Lead every thought and purpose captive to the obedience of Christ."

How do you become obedient in Christ? Think thoughts that will inspire and encourage you. Decide that you're not going to let negative thoughts roam freely in your mind.

When your mind decides that it wants to take a walk down memory lane to those past events that rendered you powerless, control it, stop it. Shout NO! Refuse to take that walk. You don't need that type of exercise. When you exercise the mind it's a process of renewal and strength. Any thought that attempts to tear you down or make you feel negative about yourself is not healthy. Shout NO!

The Bible tells us that the enemy (disguised as challenges, obstacles, and disappointments) comes to steal, kill, and destroy. The enemy wants to stop you mentally! He wants to crush your destiny. If he controls your mind, he can control your actions. The enemy wants to steal your confidence, kill your hopes, and destroy your dreams.

So many times I've tried to do something and couldn't, or it just took too long. I remember one summer I was having a bad hair day. I tried to comb my hair different ways to make it look nice, but it just wasn't cooperating. Suddenly I thought, *If you had hands, you wouldn't have this problem.* The more I combed my hair the louder this thought became. I started to get very sad, and the tears pooled in my eyes I addressed the thought saying, *You're right.* I started to go back to bed and not report to work, but then I remembered: I'm in control. I will not be defeated. I cried out, "GOD, HELP ME. I NEED A HAIR-DO SO THAT I CAN GO TO WORK."

I stood there a couple of minutes, and all of a sudden an idea came to mind. I leaned over, brushed my hair forward, twisted it around, stuck a pin in it here and there, and *voila.* I had a cute-looking up-do. I turned around and looked in the mirror to ensure that it was neat. I applied a few finishing touches and off to work I went.

I received so many compliments that day. "Karren, that hairstyle is cute." "Karren, that hairstyle brings out your face. Did Michael do that for you?" I was known to go to work with a couple of cute ponytails or twists my husband did for me. But I said, "Michael didn't do this. Me and God performed this hook-up."

It wasn't until I stopped dwelling on my situation that I heard God speak to me and give me a great idea. Occasionally, I'll still wear that hairdo and get the same reaction from people.

Your ability to move forward depends on the amount of mental time you spend dwelling on past events. How much time and energy should be wasted on these events? Very little to none! That's why you must learn how to ARM wrestle. ARM wrestling isn't a means to improve or demonstrate your brute strength but to improve your mental strength. ARM is an acronym used to describe how you should *a*ssess the situation, and *r*egain and *m*aintain control of your emotions and destiny.

17

Assess the situation to determine what happened only as a means to learn from it to ensure that it doesn't happen again. Then regain control of your emotions. Regain your strength, confidence, and courage. Tell yourself that you survived and it's time to move forward, and then maintain that position. Maintain the will to stay positive. It's almost impossible to stop our minds from replaying the past. If you do walk down memory lane, it shouldn't be to condemn and chastise. It should be a quick trip and not an everlasting journey.

You must meditate on the good to regain and maintain control of your life. This cycle will empower and propel you into the future.

Tragedy of Bitterness

A bad experience or event in our life can lead to bitterness. Bitterness can be magnified when our experience leads us to believe that God is unfair, or that our mistakes or the mistakes of others cannot be overcome. It can leave us with a loss of passion, lack of confidence, dislike for others, and most importantly dislike for ourselves.

Joyce Meyer stated it best: "Many people don't get along with themselves very well. Life is difficult if you don't get along with and accept yourself. After all, you're one person you never get away from. You're everywhere you go! If you don't get along with yourself, you won't get along with others either."

There's always something that will occur in your life that could set the stage or establish the foundation for how the rest of your life from that point forward will be. Situations or events may occur that leave you feeling guilty or like an eternal victim. You must evaluate the situation as a basis to learn and grow, instead of as a basis to self-destruct.

At some point shortly after the experience, decide what the future should look like beyond the experience. At that point your behavior will be driven by a boundary-free belief system, a belief system with no limitations, a system built on acceptance of who you are. Any belief that confines or limits your ability to propel forward or accept yourself for who you are must be eliminated. Therefore, destroy the enemy (challenges and obstacles) before it destroys you!

I learned that neither I nor my parents could change what happened. That's not to say that we didn't at times in the early years wish that my hands weren't amputated. Should I hold my parents hostage for what happened and make them feel bad for the rest of their lives? Was I going to continuously chastise myself for being an inquisitive child wanting to help my mom and at the same time nourish my curiosity? No!

I decided that who I am is not dependent on what I don't have. I decided that I wasn't bitter about an event that happened in the past. When a person is bitter they are in a mental jail. A bitter attitude affects other people. If the person is deemed the offender, then the person offended has placed them in a mental jail. The purported offender doesn't know what to say to you and how to act when they're around you.

I don't remember wanting to help wash clothes after my experience. Eventually my parents purchased an electric washing machine. My parents also didn't shelter me and decide that I would never wash clothes. No such luck. I had to learn to wash clothes just like my sister and brothers.

My dislike for washing clothes has nothing to do with my experience at the age of three. The clothes washing cycle is such a boring and repetitive process: wash, dry, and fold; wash, dry, and fold.

Life is a precious gift granted to us. I could have died that day in the hospital or days later, but I'm alive. We all have the power within us to decide our quality of life and ensure it's coupled with a positive attitude.

A positive attitude isn't boastful or arrogant but one that says to the person in the mirror, *Hey, listen up! You look good, you feel good. You're smart. You have the power to live a successful and joyous life, and you can do all things through Christ who strengthens you.* And also say to yourself, *I will be nice and kind to you today because I believe in you.*

Your experiences are less significant than how you feel on the inside after the experience, event, or situation. While that event is occurring, or even afterwards, you may feel abandoned, lonely, and discouraged. But somehow, some way, gain control and either during this event or soon thereafter say to yourself, "For He satisfies the longing soul, and fills the hungry soul with goodness" (Psalm 107:9). During or after the event, God wants to wash away your pain. He wants to wash away the hurt, the feeling of loneliness, abandonment, discouragement, and desperation. If you're reading this book, you survived!

Say out loud, *"I survived because I've been lovingly and carefully touched by the hand of God."*

You could have died or been left alone forever. But He who sits on the throne hears you and can fill your soul with joy. His hand is available to assist you and provide an abundance of strength.

As I stated earlier my dad loved to play the piano and sing. He taught us this song, which says,

All of my help, my help, my help comes from
    the Lord.
All of my help, my help, my help, comes from
    the Lord.

All of my needs and my possessions.
All of my help, my help, my help, comes from
    the Lord.
Father, I stretch my hands to thee. I know you will
    remember me.
When others forget and leave me alone, I know that
    Jesus will hear my call.

Do you have a song in your heart? Is it a song that uplifts and strengthens you? If you don't have one, get one. There are so many songs to heal and encourage you. I have a lot of favorite songs, but the best of all is the one my dad taught us years ago—all of my help comes from the Lord.

P.S. Pray and ask God to grant you peace to accept the things you cannot change. Give thanks to Him for His loving touch over your life because He cares for you.

Chapter 2

Motivated with an Attitude of Determination

CHAPTER 2

Motivation, Attitude, and Determination

*T*here he was standing by his locker surrounded by his usual group of friends. He was slender and about five-foot-five, which was the average height for eighth graders. He was talkative and well liked. A lot of kids would hang around him because he knew how to make them laugh. Even I had a chuckle or two. He was indeed the class clown.

I was hoping that I could walk right past him without being seen. But when I looked his way our eyes met. *Oh no,* I thought. *He sees me.* I could tell by the look in his eyes and the smirkish grin on his face that I was the target for that moment in time.

Just before I could dash around the hall, I heard him sing what seemed to be his daily rhythmic tune, "There goes no arms, there goes no arms." He sang this a couple of times with his arms bent and elbows held together walking toward me. Oh, how I disliked this guy. I quickened my pace and dashed into my classroom. *Whew, it's over for today*, I thought. Tomorrow though was still another day.

Have you ever had anyone tease you when you were in school? Does someone tease you now? Almost every day this boy would tease me. He would call me names and make jokes about me, and a lot of people would laugh. I never understood his need to embarrass me.

Sometimes I hated to go to school. But I knew I was smart. I was one of the best altos in the school choir. I loved to play volleyball and run track. I depended on these activities at school to keep me motivated and encouraged despite what he said. But some days I would get so upset, so angry. Why was he assigned to annoy me day after day?

Some days I felt sick and didn't want to face the jostling, humiliation, and embarrassment.

There was a time when I hoped that something would happen to him so he couldn't come to school. That was bad, but his daily abuse to me at the time was worse. Every morning I would try to think of a good comeback line. But I was too embarrassed to say anything. *Maybe one day he'll stop teasing me.*

One day I decided that regardless of what he said I was going to remain cheerful and happy. I *was not* going to allow his comments to affect me anymore. A positive attitude may not solve the problem, but I sure was going to at least feel good about myself.

It was a gloomy day—damp and windy outside. The pavements at school were wet because of the dampness. I was walking from the choir room with a group of friends, tiptoeing so that I wouldn't fall.

There he was just ahead of us going to his next class. Suddenly, without warning, he lost his balance. His books fell to the ground as he wildly swung his arms back and forth trying not to fall. It was the funniest sight to see. We laughed hysterically.

We could tell that he was embarrassed. He quickly bent over to pick up his books and paper. Just as he was rising up he saw me. *Oh shucks,* I thought. He looked at me and I knew he was going to use me as a target to divert the laughter from himself to me. "Look at you tiptoeing around," he said to me. "Look at me," I said. "I'm not the one flailing like a chicken." Our classmates laughed and surprisingly so did he. Well, needless to say the rest of the school term was great. I was determined that my need to stay positive despite his need to tease me was important.

Of course that wasn't the first or last time that people ridiculed me or attempted to embarrass me. Even today there's an odd need for someone to satisfy their insecurities or other feelings of inadequacies by verbally abusing me. But I've learned that I'm in control of my reactions. I'm in control of the emotions and attitudes that help form how I'll react in certain situations.

Has anyone ever ridiculed you? Does someone ridicule you now? How do you respond? How does it make you feel? Or maybe I should ask, "What is your attitude like?"

Use the power within you to stay happy and cheerful regardless of situations or circumstances. You're in control. Yes it's difficult but you must strive to manage your reaction to others comments. Over the years one of the most important lessons I've learned is that a fulfilling life includes a positive attitude.

Attitude

An attitude is a disposition with regard to a person or thing that is communicated verbally and non-verbally. Our attitudes are complex and diverse, generally reflecting our own differences in background, perception, and societal expectations.

Attitudes are also generally referred to as being positive or negative. You may hear someone say "She (or he) has a positive attitude." Conversely, you may hear "She (or he) has a negative attitude." Some people believe that a positive attitude guarantees success, whereas a negative attitude guarantees failure.

I know there are always points along our journey in life when we'll exemplify a negative attitude. However, we should stop and ask ourselves, "How has the journey been thus far?" When you stop and think about what has occurred in your life and how and why you're where you are today, you almost can't respond without considering how you felt.

You begin to replay in your mind significant events and reflect on your response to those events. What did you feel? What was your behavior like? Your feelings and behavior are oftentimes *driven* by your attitude.

If you're taking a road trip, it's always a good idea to either take the car to a shop to have it checked out or to check it out yourself to ensure that you make it to and from your destination safely. Now, if the engine and related systems work and you have gas in the car, it's highly probable that you'll arrive at your destination.

I'm not a mechanic but I know that a car won't operate with just an engine in place. It has to have fuel. Otherwise you won't go anywhere. Your car will stay parked in the same spot or in the garage. You purchased your car with the intent of using it, but you don't have any gas. The car must have gas with frequent fill-ups to get going and stay going.

When you do put gas in the car, the engine may operate poorly if the fuel mix is bad. If there is a bad fuel mix the car could burn fuel (gas) faster, which will result in bad gas mileage. Instead of getting 40 miles to the gallon, you may only get 30 miles per gallon.

The car could cough, sputter, and backfire. Also, the engine won't function well if there is a lack of spark. This would indicate that the spark plugs or wires are worn or weak, and it will cause the car to barely start or keep running when started.

Again, I'm not a mechanic, but basically an engine with a good fuel mix and powerful spark plugs will ensure that the car operates effectively and guarantees a safe trip. I liken our attitude to a car engine. Our attitude serves as the basis for how we function. It's a major factor in determining whether our journey will be good or not so good. If we have a negative attitude, our journey in life can be hindered and challenged, and we may find it difficult to have an emotionally healthy life. However, our attitude doesn't function alone.

Remember, a car engine is no good by itself. It must be complemented with a good fuel mix and spark plugs to facilitate a good trip; likewise our attitude doesn't function alone. Motivation and determination must complement our attitude. Actually motivation and determination form your attitude.

Motivation

Why does she eat all day? It seemed like every time I turned around she was eating. I would get full just watching her eat. Her eating habits were mysterious in a sense. I didn't want to judge her because my initial thought was that she was stressed. I was very curious. Did she eat often because she was hungry? Was she eating because she was nervous?

One day we were eating lunch. We were talking about different things—the weather, work. Finally, I mustered up enough courage to ask the question I was curious about, or maybe I was just being nosy. But it was driving me nutty! I really needed an answer.

I looked at her with a sideways glance. I had to ask the question, but I was a little afraid of what the answer might be. I just really needed to know just in case she needed a friend to talk to. I was starting to think that she'd become a stress eater.

I was hesitant and apprehensive, but I took a silent deep breath and said, "Every time I see you, you're eating." She laughed because she knew it was true. "Why do you eat so much?" I asked. "Is there something bothering you? Would you like to talk about it?"

"Well, I read an article that said we should have at least six meals a day. Eating often is supposed to help manage your sugar and cholesterol levels, so I try to eat something throughout the day," she said.

I looked at her astonished, trying not to say "Yeah right!" All I could say was "What! Sugar and cholesterol? You're kidding, right?" I laughed because I didn't expect a sugar and cholesterol managing answer. I knew what she said was true because I had read several articles on how to have a healthy heart. But this was so far removed from my idea of stress-induced overeating.

I really thought her motive for eating all day long was stress-related. Of course I told her why I thought she ate so much. We both continued to laugh. I was the one stressed, not her.

I learned that oftentimes we're not aware of why people do what they do. We're more suspicious and judgmental than knowledgeable. Sometimes we don't know why *we* do what we do.

When we think about what motivates us the answer could vary widely. What motivates a person to eat six meals a day? It depends. For my friend it was for health reasons. For another person the motive could be stress, which is what I thought was the case with my friend.

Consider another situation. Why do people go to college? What's the motive? Some may respond that they want to have a good job or increase their earning potential. Others may respond, "This is the only choice my parents gave me."

Motivation represents either your desires or the desires of others that you've adopted. It's that something on the inside that causes you to act. Sometimes we are motivated based on external factors or influences. Regardless, we must understand our motivators.

My primary motivator is achievement. To survive life's journey I believe that I can do all things through Christ who strengthens me (Philippians 4:13). This scripture energizes me! It makes we want to run forward to fulfill my desire and accomplish my goals. It actually revs me up!

If motivation is the fuel that propels you forward on your journey, could a person have bad motives? Of course. That's why I liken motivation to the fuel in your car. If your attitude is your engine and motivation is the gas, then it's important to have good fuel supporting the engine. Thus, it's good to have a good stable motive to drive your attitude just like good gas for your engine.

Think about it. When you put gas in your car what kind do you use? Well, it depends. Some people have different motives for their gas purchase. Two motives could be afford-ability or performance. With the soaring gas prices, more and more people are probably motivated by affordability. If good performance is a motive, the car owner may want to ensure that the car has a lot of power for speed and drives well.

Which motive is correct? Affordability or performance? Either one of these could be good fuel. To answer the question, a person has to determine the intent of their motive. Will the motive yield good results? If performance is the motive for power to speed on the highways, you'll exceed the speed limits—which means this is not a good motive. Power for speed that may lead to traffic tickets and possible accidents is not good. This is bad fuel!

I know you've seen them or perhaps have one yourself. Yes, I'm talking about radar detectors. Again, if performance is the motive which leads to buying a radar detector which implies that you plan to break the law, then this motive is not a good choice. Mixing the motive of performance with

31

breaking the law is not a good fuel mix. Your motive must lead to good decision making with expected positive results. But consider this. If performance is the motive because you want to ensure that the car has good power when you're commuting to and from work, easily and quickly merging into ongoing traffic, then your motive is good. Performance coupled with a comfortable commute is a good fuel mix.

Our day-to-day thought processes and attitude must be driven by the right motive. We must drive our attitude based on the right motive to help us make good decisions, and we must respond appropriately to situations and circumstances in our lives. There is something on the inside that will get us going and keep us going.

Coupled with my primary motive of achievement is perseverance. This is a good fuel mix! I'm driven to accomplish tasks and demonstrate God's Word so that I can accomplish all things. I don't give up easily. I move onward despite what is said or the obstacles in my path. The words "no" and "I can't" are not commonly used in my vocabulary. I'm motivated to demonstrate that despite what others may say or questions they may ask I must forge onward. It's satisfying to exceed your and others' expectations.

To achieve the unbelievable, I've also learned that there must be a transformation and continuous refreshing of our minds. We must believe! You can overcome and know that it's possible to overlook the ridicule of others with a positive attitude.

People have spoken words that have pierced our hearts. We cannot change how other people act and talk. The pain from their words doesn't have to linger if we learn to have the right attitude. We can only control and change ourselves. I'm amazed at how I can influence others' attitudes by managing my own.

What are your motivators? Do your motivators lead to a positive attitude and outlook on life? Paul states in Romans

12:2, "But be ye transformed by the renewing of your mind." *Our minds must be renewed!* A revival has to take place in our minds so that we can learn, grow, recover from defeat, and surmount obstacles. This can only be accomplished with a good attitude which yields a good perspective on life.

Self-preservation and love also motivate me and cause me to be enthusiastic. I can't do anything without Christ in my life. The ability to survive not based on fear but based on the love of God revs me up. It energizes me. Self-preservation combined with love is indeed a good fuel mix!

When you discover what motivates you, you'll endeavor to discover the skills and knowledge required to mature and develop. Couple your motive with a high level of *enthusiasm*. We must be excited about moving onward despite the challenges we face!

I remember the summer before I graduated from college. I applied for a clerk typist job with a government agency. I was excited about getting a job so I could start saving money for graduation. The interviewer told me that the position provided administrative assistance to one of the resource staffs.

During the interview she asked, "How fast can you type?" I suppose this was an excellent question, and for a split second I thought my chance of getting the job immediately became impossible. However, just as quickly as that thought came to mind I responded, "How soon would they need it?"

I wasn't deterred by the question during my interview. I learned that the "How fast can you type?" question was a standard interview question. The interviewer was asking everyone this question. Well, I got the job.

When I started working, I learned that the quality of the work was more important than the time. They always gave me plenty of time to type a letter or complete a form.

I never received work assignments that required me to type the information in a few minutes.

As a clerk typist, I was motivated to demonstrate that I can do all things despite the fact that I don't have hands. I knew that people would assume based on their own experiences that I couldn't write or type. Unless you've seen it or witnessed it for yourself, the idea that someone without hands can write does seem impossible.

In general, I became motivated to encourage others to believe in themselves. When I hear someone saying they can't do something, I immediately kick into gear and begin to encourage them. Sometimes I can't help myself. I become the cheerleader they never had. I become the coach challenging them to accept more and nothing less.

The guy at my junior high school tried to dampen my spirits by teasing me. That experience taught me how to overcome verbal obstacles. It taught me that the childhood saying "sticks and stones may break my bones but words will never hurt me" is untrue. Words hurt until you learn how to dismiss, ignore, and refuse to process them. Any information that will negatively impact your attitude and subsequently your behavior must be ignored.

That summer I said out loud to myself "I survived!" because I found out I didn't have to endure his behavior in high school. He went to a different high school. You too can survive when someone tries to discourage you. You can also say out loud, "I survived." Even today I have to encourage myself to survive.

Again, what is your motive? Is it self-preservation and love? What motivates you? Whatever it is hold onto it. Couple it with the Word of God, such as, "Be of good courage [confidence] and He shall strengthen your heart" (Psalm 27:14).

Pause here for a few minutes. Take the time to write down one or two things that motivate you. Don't read further. You will know you've identified it when all of a sudden you become full of energy and you're ready to put on your running shoes. When you understand what motivates you, it's hard to contain yourself. Motivation is the energy and enthusiasm to get you going. It's an ingredient to build your self-esteem by moving you into action and creating a positive attitude.

Determination

Purchasing my first car was the most exciting experience. It was a sign of freedom for me. I didn't need to negotiate around someone else's schedule. It was a sleek two-door green Buick Regal with smooth russet leather seats and interior. It was a used car, but it was in good condition. The car welcomed me as its owner as I glided over the leather seats to take it for a test drive.

As a new owner, learning to take care of my car was very important. About two years later I started having car problems. First I noticed a subtle vibration in the steering wheel. My initial reaction was that I needed a front-end alignment. However, about a month later the vibration extended from the steering wheel to the entire car. That's when I knew I had a problem and that eventually a few dollars were going to exit from my savings account.

The vibration was uncomfortable, and I was afraid my car would stop running. Sometimes when I was idle at a signal light my car would try to shut off. A few times I had to put it in park and rev the engine while I waited for the light to change. Run the air conditioner? Oh no, it would vibrate even more. This is when I knew it was time to get the car to a shop. Riding in a car with leather seats in the summertime without air conditioning wasn't my idea of fun.

I arrived at the Sears automotive center early on a Saturday morning. I had things to do that day and didn't want to be there all day. I described the symptoms, and a few hours later the diagnosis was in. The mechanic told me the car needed a tune-up; specifically, I needed to replace the spark plugs.

Spark plugs are the most important yet inexpensive operating part in a gasoline engine. The spark plugs help to ignite the air and fuel mix. The spark plugs in conjunction with other parts *fire up the engine!*

I was relieved that it wouldn't cost too much to replace the spark plugs. I was surprised that something so inexpensive would cause my car to perform poorly. The mechanic asked, "Did you notice that the car was using more gas?" No, I said. I was too focused on the vibration to notice it was using more gas.

The mechanic taught me that something as small or inexpensive as spark plugs can cause serious problems with a car. The spark plugs keep your vehicle running at peak performance. If spark plugs aren't operating sufficiently, the car will have poor gas mileage, run rough, and have poor acceleration. The car might chug along as if it were about to stop, sometimes misfiring.

If determination is absent, like spark plugs for a vehicle, you won't go anywhere or accomplish anything. You'll be like a car sitting in your garage or driveway full of gas but unable to go anywhere. You're full of motivation but can't go anywhere because you lack determination. You don't have fire! Stated differently, you have a will but no strength or energy to support your will.

Your determination is like a new set of spark plugs. It should quickly and continuously ignite and fire you up! It's the act of you making or arriving at a decision and completing your tasks and goals. That's why determination works hand-in-hand with motivation to form your attitude. Determination may seem insignificant, but it's needed to ensure that you accomplish the task and achieve your goals.

You must decide that nothing is going to stop you or cause you to misfire. Nothing is going to cause you to stay in your garage or driveway. A faulty determination will cause you to misfire and perform poorly. It will cause you to have a negative attitude; thus, you'll respond poorly and make poor decisions. Worse, you can be full of motivation but unable to keep moving because your determination needs a tune-up.

Do you need a tune-up? Does your determination need re-energizing? Have your hopes and dreams been diminished because of circumstances, events, or setbacks that have occurred in your life? Many situations can occur, such as the loss of a loved one, a divorce, inappropriate social decisions, drug or alcohol addictions, and verbal abuse. The list could go on and on. But as I stated earlier, many of these life challenges occurred in the past. Right now while you're reading this book you could be faced with one of these or other situations, but don't give up.

Deep down inside of you is the desire, the motivation, that's churning and screaming to get going, to get ready for freedom. It's waiting to be set free from the mental bondage. Motivation is ready to leap out and defeat the enemies of the past who have physically gone away but are still mentally with you.

A lady described to me a situation that happened to her twenty years ago. If she hadn't said it, I would have thought it had just happened that day. The pain in her voice and the anxiety in her expression were almost hard for me to bear. I could almost see the place as she described it, see the people, and feel the unpleasantness of the experience.

Another time I was a presenter at a training conference. I talked to the group about determination and striving onward despite the past. About a year later a lady sent me an email message about, as she described it, a horrible divorce. Her husband obtained custody of the children, and during the same time her job transferred her to a new city. She was devastated, but she remembered my telling her that she needed a determination tune-up to get going again. It was time to come face-to-face with that thing of the past, build a bridge, and get over it.

A determination tune-up is the means by which you "build a bridge and get over it." It's the time in your life when you get some new spark plugs so that you can get revved up, fired up, and re-energized. We all need a determination tune-up at different times in our lives.

I use various ways and means to get my determination fired up. First, I read the Bible and seek the Word of God for that situation. As I stated earlier my favorite scripture is Psalm 121, which states, "I will look unto the hills from whence cometh my help." The Bible has so many encouraging words for all situations in our lives. I'd suggest that you get a favorite scripture that will help you too.

My other favorite scripture reminds me that God can restore me (Psalm 23). Spend time meditating and studying the Word so that it will become engrained in your spirit and in your heart. I can be in a meeting and start saying the Word of God and get a burst of energy and joy.

Second, I spend time with people who will encourage me. I have a small family, and we're very close. I don't have to look far for a good pick-me-up because my husband has a spirit of laughter; he's a very jovial guy. My sister, who lives fifteen minutes away, is a great storyteller and can get you laughing too. They're both always encouraging me and will help to assess situations and identify solutions or just help me to build a bridge and get over it. And of course I have a few friends who are great!

Now, we all have family or friends who are naysayers. Spend less time with them when your determination is low, or learn how to filter the negative communication coming from them. Even today people are determined to tell me or gently remind me of what they think I can't do.

My husband and I went out for dinner one evening after work. I gave the cashier our credit card and waited for him to give me the receipt to sign. Instead, he gave me my receipt and told me to have a nice evening. I asked for the receipt so that I could sign it and put the tip on it. What he said next astounded me. "Ma'am, don't worry about the tip. I just scribbled your name on the receipt for you because I knew you couldn't sign it." My mouth was on the floor. But I was polite and told him I could sign it and that he should have asked.

Yes, family, friends, co-workers, and folks you don't even know will discourage you. They'll say that you shouldn't go back to school at your age. They'll say it's a dumb idea to have your own business. They'll even go to the extent of telling everyone else about what you're doing and how they don't like it to keep you down. I'm convinced that some of these people aren't consciously aware of their destructive behavior because of their own challenges.

Despite what anyone says, listen to the voice of God and your champions. They're the ones who will rev you up and get you going again. I liken them to the mechanics at the automotive stores, equipped with the right kind of tools to get the right job done, which is to get you out of the driveway and onto the streets, charged up and ready to go.

Third, I exercise and become more conscious of what I eat. It would be great if I had the discipline to exercise all the time, but I don't. However, I've learned that a little walk in the evenings makes me feel better. Okay, I know this is hard to believe but exercising gives you energy. At least it gives me energy. Also, there are certain foods I'll stop eating sometimes so that I don't feel tired and sluggish.

A determination tune-up will energize you. A tune-up will bring forth the boldness, willpower, and strength that are inside of you. Again, my determination tune-up consists of reading, studying, and meditating on the Word of God, surrounding myself with good company, and exercising.

What are some other ways you can tune-up or keep your determination charged? Write them down? How often should you do these things? Daily? Is taking an annual vacation a way to tune-up your determination?

A few years ago we decided to take a trip to a place we'd never been for a family vacation. My sister and her family and my husband and I would either visit my mom in Louisiana every year, or my mom and brothers would come to visit us in Maryland. To all of us this was boring. So we decided to plan an annual family get-together.

The first year we went to Las Vegas. No, we're not gamblers. There are so many non-gambling things to do in Vegas and the surrounding areas: Hoover Dam, Lake Meade, Red Rock Canyon, Cirque-du-Soleil shows, rollercoaster riding, and on and on. We had a blast! The next year we cruised to the Bahamas. Changing our vacation plans energized us.

Often we don't feel charged up because of fear. Fear has caused many people to lose sight of what really matters in life. But this is the time when you must move forward.

The ability to achieve the unbelievable is based on your determination.

Motivated with an Attitude of Determination

Have you ever had a meal that was "slap-scrumptious"? I mean a meal that makes your mouth water hours later just thinking about how good it was. A meal that makes you want to slap your knee because it was so good. Well, I cooked a casserole one night and it was slap-scrumptious. It was absolutely fantastic. Of course I had leftovers, which was great for me.

The next day I took my lunch to work—a nice helping of the slap-scrumptious casserole. Twelve o'clock couldn't come fast enough. My mouth watered as I walked down the hall humming a song. I was in for a treat. I could hardly wait for the savory aroma to saturate the hallways and office because I knew people were going to ask, "What is that smelling so good?"

I had to go through a set of double doors to use the microwave in the lounge. I was holding my food with both arms so I had to use my right hip to press the bar on the door and then lean into it to open it. The door was heavy so I had to give it a good push when I leaned into it so that it would swing open, giving me enough time to quickly walk through. I learned this door-opening technique because this was the same path I used to meet with other staff members, and I'd always be holding papers or carrying binders.

I put my food in the microwave and set the timer for a few minutes. I savored the aroma while I waited for the food to warm up. When the microwave stopped, I could barely contain myself. I thought I was going to salivate from the aroma.

I grabbed my dish out of the microwave and proceeded back to my office. As I approached the door, I realized that I had a problem. I couldn't open the door and hold my food at the same time. The only other way to my office posed the same problem. The door didn't have a handicap button to push or a sensor to open automatically. Also, there wasn't a window in the door so I could see if someone was approaching from the other side. The technique I used to get in wasn't what I could use to go out.

I stood there for the longest time, waiting for someone to come through and open the door. After about five minutes I decided to try and open the door myself. I was hungry and had a date with my slap-scrumptious casserole.

I took my dish and placed it against my side with my left arm. The door was very heavy, and it took a considerable amount of effort to pull it open. But I was able to quickly swing it open with my right arm. As soon as I opened the door I had to release it and grab my dish because it was beginning to slip off my waist. Just when I thought I had successfully made it through, the door swung shut and hit me hard on my behind, propelling me forward. It happened so fast I didn't have a chance to react. All I knew was that my lunch, the slap-scrumptious casserole from the previous night, was splattered all over the floor.

I just stood there. I didn't know whether to cry or faint. I stood there looking at my broken dish and my food splattered on the floor. A wave of sadness started to overwhelm me. I was beginning to feel sorry for myself. I wondered if this would have happened if I had hands. Would my food be on the floor? Wouldn't I be at my desk enjoying my meal by now if I had just one hand?

I was very upset as I kneeled down on the floor to clean up the mess. Finally, a few people came by but it was too late. I was embarrassed, and they could tell I was hurt. A few offered to buy my lunch or bring me something back from the sandwich shop or other places downtown, but I'd lost my appetite.

As I dwelled on what happened my emotions went from utter disgust to raging anger. I was fired up and mad. I was mad at myself. Mad at the door. Mad at the building owners for creating the ridiculously heavy doors. I was mad, mad, mad! I wanted to go home. I barely got any work done the rest of that day. I was so upset that even when the hunger pangs returned, I was too stubborn to satisfy myself with even a bag of chips.

I felt like I was on a roller coaster that was only traveling downward. The feeling in the pit of my stomach was nauseating, and my thoughts of myself were disgusting. I was allowing that single incident to damage my self-esteem. My confidence was declining. I even started questioning why I had moved to North Carolina. Why did I want to be an accountant? Why? Why? Why? Questions unrelated to what had just occurred maybe ten minutes prior.

Asking myself a series of unrelated questions somehow fed my need to have a successful pity party. I even asked the other "Why?" but I couldn't finish that question, not even in my mind. I stopped it right in its tracks. I couldn't let that question join my mental pity party. That question wasn't allowed. Surely I wasn't going to ask myself "Why don't I have hands?"

Finally, my work day was over. Later on I decided to assess what happened. What could I have done differently to open the door? Hold my lunch on the right side and open with my left arm? Should I have walked back to the lounge and asked someone to open the door? I wrote down the word *mad*. Then I wrote it over and over. The more I wrote the word the harder I pressed with the pen.

Eventually my sadness turned to joy because what seemed a bad word formulating a terrible feeling of low self-esteem and zero confidence turned into something positive. I'd learned the secret to stopping the pity party.

Instead of looking at the word as an adjective, I converted it to an acronym. Ah-ha! Finally, I got it. I know what it can be. How could I forget my own lesson? The things I would tell other people to do I wasn't applying in my own life. MAD! I shouted just to see what kind of reaction I would get for myself based on the tone and pitch in my voice. Saying "I'm MAD!" with a smile was kind of awkward, but I kept saying it. I modified my facial expression to correlate with the inflection, giving the word MAD a cheerful and more empowering sound.

I finally decided that I liked it. It was catchy and uplifting. MAD is an acronym for Motivated with an Attitude of Determination. Notice that the word *attitude* in MAD is flanked by motivation and determination. The word *attitude* is intentionally in the middle. An imbalance in our attitude influences our motivation and level of determination. It's rare that you see a person with a negative attitude who is motivated and determined.

A negative attitude can drive a high level of motivation and determination, but does it lead to overall good decision making? Does a negative attitude facilitate positive self-esteem, confidence, and courage? My experience is that it doesn't.

You may have never dropped a plate of food. Or, if you have, the result didn't unearth your mental foundation. But have you ever had an event occur in your life whose outcome was devastating? The outcome, though minor or insignificant to others, was heart-wrenching for you because it tugged at the core of your hurt or past pains.

The outcome caused you to dwell on the past events in your life and question the events or subsequent decisions. Have you ever had a pity party with *me, myself, and I?* Asking yourself questions that you knew would cause you to feel lowly, helpless, and despondent?

For a short period of time I wondered about the expertise of the doctors who treated me when my hands got stuck in the wringer of the washing machine. Did they know what they were doing? Did they seek advice from others in their profession?

What questions have you asked yourself? Would I still be married if…? Would I always have inappropriate relationships if…? Would I have a better paying job if…? Would I have this much debt if…? Would I be promiscuous if…? Would I use drugs if…?

If you have a long-term negative reaction to a situation or experience, your attitude affects you more than it does others. People generally move on without knowing that what they've said or done has negatively affected you. They move on with their life while you continue to dwell on the situation and allow it to affect your next steps and even your future.

The questions could go on and on. And any of these questions could have been triggered by a single event—the event that, although unrelated on the surface, still strikes at the core of your previous pain. Just when you thought you were okay with what happened you discover that you're not healed or recovered.

How exhausting it would be if we walked around backwards all day long. It would be as if you were walking into the past or staying in the same spot, predicament, or situation. In other words, you would be stuck because rather than walking forward you would constantly be stepping into the past.

Think about it. You'd have to continuously look over your shoulders to ensure that you didn't bump into anything. You wouldn't make as much progress because that's not how we're naturally designed to move around. You would tire sooner and become very annoyed. People would ask a lot of questions, including the obvious: "Why are you walking backwards? Why are you dwelling in the past?"

Motivated with an Attitude of Determination will cause you to say, "I'm determined to succeed and not fail. I'm determined to take control of my attitude and my emotions. I'm going to press forward and not backwards."

Being Motivated with an Attitude of Determination, or in short MAD, will cause you to stop the force of your subconscious. MAD will stand at the conscious gate of your mind and dispel any questions, ideas, and thoughts that attempt to rob you of your joy. It will stop the force of the subconscious to resurface the events of the past because the ability to be MAD will disempower the will to be sad. It will cause you to decide that a pity party is a waste of energy and time!

The same energy and time spent being mad is converted to an investment of energy and time to be glad. You'll be Motivated with an Attitude of Determination instead of an attitude of destruction. The Bible admonishes us to consider it all joy when we face trials (James 1:1) because these are opportunities for us to learn and grow and conform into His image (Romans 8:28-29, James 1:2-3.) I've noticed that a lot of people with negative attitudes are that way because of their past or current experiences. I've heard stories of neglect and abuse. These experiences generally trigger negative emotions. We must exercise the power to choose a positive attitude for life's challenges. We must choose a courageous attitude, an attitude that will lead to victories and not defeats, hopefulness and not helplessness. Our attitude governs how we perceive the world and how the world perceives us. We can't perceive the world as a scary place to live where people are out to get us. We must perceive the world as a place with challenges that are good but at times may be bad.

During the bad times we must continue to hold onto our convictions and beliefs. The Bible tells us to count it all joy even when it's hard to (James 1:1.) Your situation may not be the best, but you're still alive and thus you survived, so think and be positive.

Some days we have to take a step at a time or one day at a time. And these progressive forward-moving moments will eventually lead to total forgiveness and healing. Most importantly, these moments will lead to an improved means of ensuring that despite the challenges, large or small, that may occur in your life, you own the responsibility to take control of your future and destiny.

I've learned to use two very powerful influences over my attitude and my emotions: self-talk and self-acceptance. Self-talk helps me assert control over my life, primarily how I respond to others and to situations. Self-acceptance says that I'm uniquely designed and beautifully made, reaffirming the saying that "God don't make no junk."

Self-Talk

I've talked to a lot of people about attitudes and how they affect our journey in life. The gist of our conversations has been that it's hard for some people to adjust their attitudes because they believe it requires a total change. They believe it requires them to give up who they are. However, creating an attitude of change helps create a positive "can do" spirit. Change begins in our heart and in our minds.

Self-talk is the internal dialogue that takes place in our minds. The main voice we listen to is our own. Besides God, you are your strongest mentor, coach, and friend.

Positive self-talk will help in times of hardship and challenges. Just when we think we can't go on because the burden or obstacle is too heavy or too much to overcome, our inner self says, "You can do this."

When we look at our situation as being too heavy we give up because we start to project and assess our ability to carry it. However, positive self-talk lifts your spirit and encourages you. It will cause you to reassess the weight of your burden and decide that the burden is actually light.

I often use the Scriptures to motivate me. When doubt attempts to discourage your actions and cause anxiety and fear, replace the thoughts in your mind and meditate on what is good. This method can be used for any situation whether self-imposed or imposed by others.

A guy told me one day, "My wife says that you should wear long-sleeved shirts. Your arms look funny when you wear a sleeveless shirt." Now, I admit that I was offended. However, via self-talk I reminded myself of God's Word, which says I'm fearfully and wonderfully made (Psalm 139:14). God carefully and skillfully made me. I'm satisfied in knowing that His craftsmanship extended outside of my mom's womb. Thus, I feel good about whose I am and how I look. So you and I can say to ourselves, "Boy, do I look good."

People have said things to you as well. What amazes me is that they say these things out loud. My goodness, do you have any respect for the other person's feelings? Well, some folks don't. It's your responsibility not to accept the negative things that other people say and do. Again, it's your responsibility. Control yourself. Decide to leave the negative comments or actions with the person who delivered it or, if self-imposed, leave it where it should be.

When you have the right attitude you're not totally focused on what people say and do. You don't focus on or meditate on the burden or obstacle that is too heavy or too much to overcome. Focus on how you will strengthen yourself, how you can become stronger. Focus on what you need to do to get stronger so that you can either carry the load or get rid of it, because giving up is not an option. Say out loud, "GIVING UP IS NOT AN OPTION."

You can strengthen yourself in various ways. In this case I'm referring to mental strength instead of physical strength. Your brain is a thinking organ that learns and grows through perception and action. Therefore, you can teach it to be MAD. You can mentally stimulate your brain by thinking and doing positive things.

Change some of your daily habits to teach yourself how to appreciate life. For example, listen to music. Try listening to a genre different from the usual, such as jazz. Stop and smell the flowers. It's amazing how the aroma deflects you. This is an unusual step or process for many people.

Read positive or thought-provoking books or poetry. Instead of driving by the park, stop and take a walk. While walking, listen to the sound of the wind, birds, and trees. Yes, the trees make a lot of noise, and they're just beautiful to watch. I've sat many times and watched the birds, squirrels, and butterflies play.

Have you ever heard someone laugh so hard that it brought a smile to your face? Learn to focus on the laughter of others. Even when you don't know what's funny, it'll still bring a smile to your face. It's great seeing people with large smiles on their faces and belly-bending/knee-slapping laughter in their hearts. Laughter is contagious.

Train yourself to dwell on what's good instead of what's bad. I like to watch television because certain programs are entertaining or a de-stressor for me. However, there are certain programs I don't watch because they'll cause me to internalize or negatively relate the situation to my own life. Therefore, learn what programs not to watch or watch less television altogether.

Self-Acceptance

Self-acceptance can be influenced by what we see or hear. Many people measure themselves by what other people look like including their size, height, or style of dress. This is why so many people go on unhealthy diets as a means of getting immediate results to measure up to what others look like. You must embrace your meticulous design and uniqueness, not others'.

Some people grow up in a non-nurturing environment, or perhaps they are currently in one. In addition, some people, because of their own lack or feeling of insignificance, make it their goal in life to ensure that others around them feel the same way.

Telling people they're beautiful, they're smart, complementing them on things they've done regardless of how great or small is important. Giving accolades can be so easy, but it's difficult for many people because it requires them to move from a self-focus and show love and kindness to others.

We must surround ourselves with people who are sincerely interested in our health and welfare. If you receive positive feedback and imbed that within your heart and spirit, you can excel.

Even though what we hear and what we see can influence how we feel, we must be aware that accepting ourselves is our responsibility. We can't delegate the responsibility of self-acceptance. We must learn to accept who we are. Speak positively to yourself. Sometimes I stand in front of a mirror and force myself to look at every inch of my body. I literally go on a reconnaissance mission. During that mission I tell myself that I'm beautiful, that I'm beautifully made, that I'm a child of God, and that He doesn't make junk. I tell myself how much I love me and how great it is to be alive and well. I tell myself that life is great because I want it to be and that no one can stop me. I tell myself that I'm the master of the ship, the co-captain, doing my part to ensure that my ship stays afloat.

I'm motivated when I hear someone say they can't do something. That stirs me up and sets me into an exhortation mode to encourage them to think *I can* instead of *I can't*. Without realizing it they become a champion for themselves. Sometimes we have to teach people how to be their own champions.

Do you become discouraged when you're not immediately successful in your attempts to accomplish a goal? You always know when a person dreads discouragement when they use the word *but*. For example, a person may desire to go to school and get a bachelor's degree, or to get a job promotion. However, when you talk to them they say, "I would go back to school, but I made a C in the English class. I would apply for that position, but I probably wouldn't get selected because I'm not as qualified."

Discouragement and the dread of discouragement cause us to evade our goals, evade our responsibilities, and short-circuit our dreams. Discouragement causes us to see ourselves for less than we really are.

Don't be discouraged and give up on your goals! Press forward focused on satisfying God and yourself. How healthy is your attitude about yourself? Do you view challenges as opportunities to improve how or what you think about yourself? Let's ensure that challenges are viewed as opportunities to help you accomplish your plans to accept who you are. If you don't like the present, you have the opportunity to mold your future.

The present isn't deemed in terms of time but in terms of who you are. What do you look like? How are you shaped or made? Apple? Pear? Who cares? Many people focus on the wrong thing anyway. Are you healthy is the real question. Just because the left tooth is longer than the right one is irrelevant. Just because you weigh one hundred pounds more than your friend is irrelevant.

Embrace you! I could lose a few pounds, but it's not because of what others think. It's because it's hard for me to do certain things when I gain more weight. For example, it's hard for me to tie my shoes if I have more weight around my stomach. For some people this isn't a problem; however, I don't have hands and forearms, and so therefore my reach is shorter. I need to minimize how much weight I gain in my midriff so that I can bend over and do things. I don't lose or try to maintain my weight because of the beauty of someone else.

My motive to lose weight or tone my muscles is because of the abilities I need to do certain things as opposed to how I compare to other people. Always assess your motives. Don't live your life comparing yourself to others. I've learned that if you actually knew or understood others' challenges, you'd be happy with yourself rather than wish you were like someone else.

What are your wonderful qualities? Do you have beautiful hands? I've seen men and women alike with beautiful hands—no scars, well manicured, and smooth. I've seen women with naturally long eyelashes or beautiful facial skin.

51

I've seen long and short marvelous hairstyles. I myself have beautiful long legs.

Does someone else's opinion matter? Should they agree with your assessment? No. I love my legs and I keep a nice pedicure to ensure I have a complementary accent from my feet to my legs. I don't focus on the fact that I don't have hands for a manicure. I don't dwell on what I can't change because it's a waste of time and energy. Therefore, don't waste your time either. Focus on what you have and work it!

P.S. Remember, you're in control of improving yourself and accomplishing your goals and dreams by being Motivated with an Attitude of Determination (MAD). Don't give up. We succeed based on the strength of our will.

Chapter 3

I can do it, I can do it.
Yes I can, yes I can!

CHAPTER 3

Yes I Can, Yes I Can

❧

Learning to Drive

*O*ur age is sometimes used to recall significant events in our lives. The age of thirteen identifies you as an entry level teenager (I was told that the age of fourteen identifies you as an official teenager). However, it was the marvelous age of sixteen that I looked forward to. On October 1, I could get my driver's license. This was a major milestone, a major accomplishment. Just imagine, me learning how to drive! *I can do it, I can do it. Yes I can, yes I can!* On January 1 of that year I knew I had to develop a plan to ensure that I accomplished that goal.

Driver's education classes were being offered that summer. I had prayed about this opportunity all year. So why not learn how to drive? I would be able to drive to the movies and other places. I had things to do and places to go. The public bus wasn't always a convenient mode of transportation. Walking was good at times, but when you were in your best outfit, walking wasn't the coolest option, especially in the summer.

That night at the age of fifteen, during the summer before my sixteenth birthday, I said my prayers and ended by saying, "Lord, I want to learn how to drive. Please make the doctor in New Orleans sign the consent form so that I can take the driver's education class."

The doctor was hesitant about signing the form because I had stopped wearing the prostheses, but he signed anyway. I was so excited and yet surprised. I shouldn't have been surprised because I had prayed about it. I still hadn't learned and fully comprehended that the Lord always answers prayers as long as it is according to His will.

I took a copy of the signed form to my high school to register for the driver's education class. They scheduled me to take class every Saturday morning for six weeks. That Friday night I could hardly sleep. I tossed and turned, excited about the next day.

I got up early Saturday morning to eat breakfast so I wouldn't be late. I visited with myself in the mirror and said, "Well, girl, you're going to take your first driving class today. Aren't you excited? Aren't you thrilled? Now go and do a good job. Pay attention and listen carefully to the instructor. Be nice to yourself."

My mom took me to school that morning. A student from my school signed up for the Saturday morning class as well. The instructor asked, "Who's first?" Of course I said that I was first. I had a natural desire to take the lead and set the pace. My spirit just didn't like second place too often. I always liked setting the pace, establishing the parameters and guidelines.

I got into the front seat and fastened my seat belt. Then I sat there with the biggest smile on my face waiting for the instructor. It was so quiet in the car. I sat there thinking that he was thinking about where we were going. So I patiently waited for his instructions.

Finally, I noticed in my peripheral vision that he was looking at me. I turned and looked at him and kept smiling. But he kept looking at me as if he wanted to ask me a question but didn't quite know what to say. It finally dawned on me that he noticed I didn't have hands. He was probably thinking, *What am I going to do? She doesn't have any hands! She can't drive!*

But I looked at him and conveyed these thoughts: *Look here, buddy. You're part of the Master's plan to teach me how to drive. I know I'm new information to you. But have faith. I've prayed about this too long and had to endure that humiliating experience with those doctors and all those other folks in New Orleans. I'm not getting out of this car. Get yourself together and let's go. It's not my fault that God didn't forewarn you.*

I continued to smile and looked in the back seat where the other lady sat. I thought again, *Hear ye, hear ye, you have a dilemma. She can't drive either. You're the only one who can drive. So get yourself together and let's get going.* I turned around and faced forward again. Eventually the instructor told me to start the car and gave me my first driving lesson.

At the end of the six-week session, I was the best driver of the two of us. Whenever the other girl would drive, the instructor and I would look at each other and exhale. We were nervous when she drove. I succeeded and didn't allow anyone else's plans to stop me from accomplishing my goal of learning how to drive. I had prayed about it and that was it. My mom was glad when I received my driver's license. I became the family chauffeur, and eventually she was comfortable enough to let me drive without her. Soon I graduated to driving to the movies and other places. Wow, this was great!

Become a Driver

I soon realized why I was so excited about driving. I defied the law established in the minds of many people, which is "If you don't have hands you can't drive." I had also encouraged myself and helped others realize that if it's to be it's up to me.

Learning to drive enlarged my territory and created opportunities to go beyond my boundaries. I was no longer limited by my mom's schedule, where the public transportation could get me, or where my legs could take me. When you learn to drive, you can go to places you've never gone before.

Learning to drive put me in control of where I wanted to go and when I wanted to get there. If you rely on public transportation, a lot of time is spent getting to your destination because the buses or any other transportation operates on a set schedule, a time frame established by others. If you are the driver it could take fifteen minutes to get to your destination, whereas if you're being driven it may take twice the amount of time, or thirty minutes.

There was a snowstorm in Maryland one night, and the next day I decided to ride the bus instead of drive to the metro station. I reviewed the schedule and gave myself enough time to walk to the bus stop. The bus meandered through many neighborhoods picking up people, many who also decided to ride instead of drive. It took about thirty minutes to get to the metro station. Even on a snowy day it still would have taken me half the time to arrive at the station.

Or if you ask someone to take you to your destination, unbeknownst to you there are additional stops they're going to make. Just when you've estimated the amount of time it'll take to reach your destination, you find it will now take longer because the driver has imposed their agenda. Thus, you're on their time and not your own.

You may not know how to drive a car; however, the driving experience can be applied to our life—namely, to be in control of where you're going and when you need to get there in terms of your goals and aspirations.

The term *driving* isn't limited to the use of transportation but is also used to indicate the action taken to move forward. The word *driving* is used to identify a person's personality. Have you heard someone say, "She has a driving personality"? They're saying that an individual is energetic, enterprising, and urging. A driving personality demonstrates that you're willing to exert the effort required to ensure that you succeed. A driving personality indicates that you're no longer in park or sitting idle.

What are your goals? Were they set by you or someone else? Who's directing when these goals will be accomplished? Most importantly, who's driving?

When you're the driver, you are in control of the steering wheel, the gas pedal, and the brake. Therefore, you're in control of where you are going and the turns you will need to take to get there. Most importantly, you control the gas pedal, which will regulate your pace and the timing of your arrival, or when the goal is accomplished. Will you need to make stops along the way? Yes, and thus you're in control of the brakes, knowing when to slow down and when to actually stop.

Get started. It's time to move your goals from park or idle to drive. You're the driver! Don't wait for the bus to pick you up; drive yourself.

Getting Behind the Wheel

When you start driving, you must ensure that you're prepared. The ability to get from where you are now to where you should be requires you to concentrate not only on your driving responsibilities but also the proper driving techniques.

Proper driving techniques include having a good sitting position and steering control. These techniques are important when you drive. If you're not sitting properly, you won't have ultimate control of the car. When you're not in control of the car, you won't be able to handle the bumps or obstacles in your path, and you may become prematurely tired while driving. Also, the steering wheel provides feedback about the road surface as communicated by the tires and brakes.

Likewise, when you're on your path of success to accomplish your goals, you'll need proper techniques to succeed. Are you in the right position? What feedback have you received based on the route you're taking to accomplish your goals?

First, you must get in the right position. The right position is the knowledge and understanding of your purpose. It's your purpose that defines what you do and how you think and feel. Your purpose helps establish your goals.

Do you know your purpose? What were you created to do? I was talking to a lady one day, and she told me that she wanted to go to school and become a nurse. She said that this had always been her dream. We talked for several minutes. She finally realized why she didn't like her current job. Her job as a secretary didn't align with what she was supposed to do.

I've talked to a lot of people who are very frustrated in their current jobs. I enjoy my job as an accountant, but I have greater pleasure in helping people set goals and seek after their true desire and passion.

When you discover your purpose, you'll then need to "Write the vision and make it plain on tablets, that he may run who reads it" (Habakkuk 2:2). Write down the vision for your purpose. Establish goals or major milestones to ensure that you're successful.

For example, let's say that you have an assignment to drive from Maryland to Southern California. What will you do? Will you just get in your car and start driving? I hope not. You'll need to map out a course or plan to get from Maryland to California. Are you driving or flying? When will you leave? Are you returning? If so, when? If not, where are you going to live in California? Also, what city in California are you going to?

Without a plan, will you get to California? No. You need a plan. Otherwise, it will take much longer to reach your destination and you may become distracted and lose focus. It may take longer to get there because you got lost along the way, you didn't plan for inclement weather (you didn't consider the time of year so you may have traveled through snowy or icy states), or you didn't properly plan for rest and relaxation for your journey. Also, if you don't write down your plans you may become distracted and get off course.

Likewise, let's say that you want to start a business. Have you conducted research? What's the best location? Who are your potential clients? Do you have a business plan? You must have a written plan which will serve as your map or course of action. Your business plan coupled with your research and analysis will help position you for success.

When I wrote down my goals a few years ago, I immediately got charged up. I was energized and ready to get started. All of a sudden my goals became real and urgent. Writing my goals served as a confirmation that these were the items required to fulfill my purpose in life. Thus, your written goals help you focus.

I currently work for the federal government as an accountant. I've been tempted to take offers to earn more money by either changing agencies or working for a private firm. However, each time I must remind myself of my overall purpose. Although the extra income would be nice, it isn't part of the overall plan and would distract me.

If I was to take another job I could possibly work more hours or be under more stress, which would distract me or make me more tired. Your strength should be reserved to fulfill your purpose in life, to help you do what you were created to do. Ensure that you understand your purpose so that you're firmly positioned for your journey. Also, to get in the right position, create your own style. Don't imitate others. Many people have similar goals, but the style or task required to accomplish the goal and be successful will vary. For example, I'm going to be a world-renowned inspirational speaker. When I went to a seminar several years ago the speaker was fantastic. His primary prop was a chair. He would step up and down on the chair throughout his presentation. So I decided that I'd add props to my presentation to give it additional excitement and enthusiasm.

I was so exhausted trying to mimic his style that during my presentation I was constantly out of breath. I was tired! I struggled with trying to breathe smoothly and present my information. I finally decided that this was not my style.

Likewise, your goal could be to start your own restaurant. Will your menu consist of a few specialty items that you know you're good at cooking and can teach others to cook, or will it consist of one hundred items with no specialty? One of the things that attract most people to a restaurant is specialty items. Create your own style for success.

Paul stated to the people of Corinth in 1 Corinthians 11:1, "Imitate me, just as I also imitate Christ." He was stating that we should only use him as an *example* in attempting to model ourselves after Christ. Thus, when you create your own style, don't imitate others but imitate Christ. Christ is so creative that He'll help you establish your own style.

Another proper driving technique is to be in control of your steering. When you're driving a car, the tires and brakes provide feedback to the steering wheel about the road conditions. That feedback lets you know whether you're experiencing a rough or smooth ride.

Many times when people are driving they're gripping the steering wheel tightly thinking that this will give them maximum control. In actuality it won't because a tight grip indicates that you're not relaxed and capable of properly handling the various road conditions without overreacting. You must learn to relax when you're driving so that you're sensitive to road conditions and don't overreact.

Likewise, when we're on the road to fulfill our goals, we must be as relaxed as possible. Yes, there are times when our intensity level will be high, but being in a relaxed or calm state of mind will help control our steering, the direction we're going. Controlling our steering will help us to properly respond to the various challenges that we face. If you're always tense, you may over or improperly react to certain situations, and your faith may subsequently be diminished.

God rules the raging of the sea when the waves rise, and He calms it (Psalm 89:9). God will bring calmness to your situations and bestow upon you peace to endure the ride. He'll bring calmness to your journey to ensure that your overall experience is smooth.

There are many responsibilities that come with driving a car. The primary responsibility is to show love. Love is exemplified by being courteous, kind, and respectful. Just like driving, be courteous because you can help avoid accidents and keep traffic moving in an orderly fashion. You're not the only one on the road! Others will be impacted by your decision. Therefore, be familiar with God's laws and rules.

Think and Say "I Can"

Willie A. Young, a painter, asked his little girl many years ago how to spell the word *can't* because she had a tendency to use it a lot. When she spelled the word he told her it was incorrect and that there was no such word. Well, that little girl was me. I thought I was the smartest girl this side of heaven.

Each week my siblings and I were assigned a different chore to do. There were just certain duties I didn't like, such as mopping the floor or washing dishes. Whenever it was my turn to wash dishes I would try to get out of doing the chore. I'd go to my dad and say, "Daddy, I can't wash the dishes." Every time I told him I couldn't do something he would ask me to spell the word *can't*. I would respond, "C, A, N, apostrophe, T."

I was proud of myself because I was smart in school, an excellent speller, and I knew that correctly spelling the word *can't* was my ticket from the chore for that week. I was beaming. Then of all things that could have ever come out of my dad's mouth he told me I had spelled the word incorrectly. *What?* I thought. *Is he insane?* I was crushed. Of course that was how you spelled the word. What was he thinking?

On the next chore rotation I decided to try it again. "Dad, I can't do that chore." And he asked me to spell the word *can't*. This time I was ready. I had thought it out. This time I slowly spelled the word. I was hoping that the last time I spelled the word I had spelled it too fast and he just didn't understand me.

At the time, I was about five feet three inches tall. I stood up straight with my chest extended because this was a serious matter. Properly spelling the word meant more playtime for me, not just for now but forever. Instead of washing dishes or mopping floors I could be playing with my dolls.

I was taught in school that you always say the word first and then spell it. I stood up straight, cleared my throat, and said, "Can't." Then I slowly spelled it, "C, A, N, apostrophe, T, can't." My dad looked at me and said, "That's not how you spell the word." I ran and grabbed the dictionary. I frantically flipped through the pages looking for the word and said, "See? Here it is. That's how you spell the word *can't*."

He looked at me calmly and said, "No, that's not how you spell the word because there's no such word as can't. I don't know who put it in the dictionary. People are just making up stuff. I'll write Webster and tell them to take this word out of the dictionary."

Regardless of what I said, his position was the same and I had to complete my chores. It didn't take long to learn that going to him for release from my chores was absolutely a waste of time. My dad was determined to teach me how to succeed.

The word *can't* is in the dictionary; however, it's not an empowering word. We have the power to determine the words that will be part of our vocabulary. We have the full authority to determine the words that will be part of our self-development, words that we can grab hold of to encourage, motivate, or serve as an inspiration.

The word *can't* wasn't a word my dad wanted me to include in my vocabulary because he knew that you can become what you think. If you think you can't, then you won't. If you think you can, then you will.

Self-imposed verbal limitations deal with our ability to place boundaries, restrictions, and confinements on ourselves. This isn't to say that other people don't impose limitations for us or set boundaries, but I want to focus on what we tend to do ourselves.

People can attempt to discourage you or not provide positive feedback or constructive criticism that can help you grow; however, it's up to you to accept or decline someone's comments or statements. Others can stop us temporarily, but we're the only ones who can stop ourselves permanently. What are you really capable of accomplishing? No one knows, including you.

You don't really know what you're capable of doing until you try and try and try again. Someone told me a story about the strength of elephants. An elephant can pick up a one-ton load with his trunk. But have you ever visited a circus and watched these huge elephants standing quietly tied to a small wooden stake?

While still young and weak, an elephant is tied by a heavy chain to an immovable iron stake. No matter how large and strong he becomes he continues to believe he cannot move as long as he sees the stake in the ground beside him. Many intelligent adults also behave like this. They may not be physically tied to a heavy chain but may be mentally restrained by their thoughts and actions.

Believe that you can do what you desire to accomplish. Think and say "I can." Don't use the words "I can't" as part of your daily vocabulary because that mindset will inadvertently change or set the pace for your life's journey.

Shout these words out loud: "I can do it, I can do it. Yes I can, yes I can!" You're the driver now. Your goals can only be accomplished when you position yourself and take control of the steering wheel. You're equipped with some basic tools to get you started and on your way. You can do it, you can do it. I know you can!

Summertime

"We are fine, we are great. We are seniors of seventy-eight. We are FINE, we are GREAT. We are SENIORS OF SEVENTY-EIGHT. WE ARE FINE, WE ARE GREAT. WE ARE SENIORS OF SEVENTY-EIGHT!" We were in the school gym. Each class was yelling loud trying to outdo the other with its class chant. Of course, we were the loudest because this was the last day of school. In a few months we would be seniors! I was looking forward to working that summer. It was my first job and I was excited.

I worked in the recreation department at the state school for disabled children and adults. This was a great job because I was able to work inside during the hot summer days in

Louisiana and periodically go outside to take the residents to the park and play games. When the summer job was coming to a close, I knew that in a few weeks I'd be entering high school as a senior.

I was talking with some of the employees when one of the ladies asked me what I was going to do after I graduated from high school. I told them I was going to college and major in accounting. I was excited about my senior year because I was accepted to attend classes at the magnet high school and take pre-college courses.

I had registered for an accounting class just to ensure that it was the degree I wanted to pursue. However, when I said that I was going to college, one of the ladies looked at me and said, "College? Yeah, right. You can't go to college. You'll be living off of Social Security the rest of your life." I looked at her and said, "Social Security? Social security can't pay me the money I need to buy the things I want and go to places I want to go." I was appalled. How dare she make a comment like that to me? Apparently she didn't understand that I was a smart girl with great expectations. I thought maybe she wasn't thinking clearly because of the summer heat.

People often tell you what you can't do because they don't see themselves achieving or accomplishing that same goal. This lady had never gone to college. The idea that I was considering education beyond high school was unimaginable for her.

The problem is that a lot of people compare themselves to others. They assess the other person's qualities, good or bad, and measure themselves against their assessment. But in this case I was measured against her low expectations of herself. Thus, she attempted to impose those expectations on me.

Many people don't like to accept the expectations others have for themselves, because then it may indicate to them that they're a failure. What many people don't realize is that it's more important to embrace your own uniqueness as demonstrated in your gifts and talents. People are needed in various positions to perform various duties in all kinds of organizations. Embracing your own gifts and talents will ensure that you're successful in your plans for life.

Your Thoughts and Feelings Create Your Experience

Your underlying thoughts and feelings are conveyed by how you express yourself in words and actions. Others' underlying thoughts about you are irrelevant if the basis of their thought is to keep you from progressing and living a successful life.

Change your verbal patterns if you find yourself always saying negative things. Don't give place to negative thoughts because if you keep saying you can't, then you won't. Your past experience can also affect your expectations.

I knew that I wanted to learn how to drive. At that time in my life, my only plans were to run errands for my mom, go to the movies, and meet my friends at the mall. That was as far as my thoughts went. But I couldn't allow what other people thought to dictate how I felt about myself and what I was going to accomplish. I knew that I had asked God if I could drive, that I had expressed a desire to go to school, and in both cases He said yes. No one else's opinion or thoughts mattered.

Suppose you've been practicing for months to run in a marathon. You get to the race and see the other runners. You line up. The gun fires and you start running. About five miles later, you begin to think negative things such as, *That runner is fit and trim. I can't win against them; I'm going to finish last. Why did I do this?* You begin to run slower. Your thoughts create a negative experience because you're telling yourself that you're a loser. Whereas you could say, *Wow, they're fit and trim, but so am I. I can win. I'm going to make it to the finish line.*

For you, it may not be running a race. But what is it? Is it that you want to get a college degree but you and others have been saying you'll never finish just because you haven't completed any previous task? Is it that the people you're talking to don't have a degree and thus don't want you to have one? Is it that you can't possibly start and succeed in your own business because you've seen what has happened to others? Whatever your desire, believe that you can do it. Be in control of your experience from this point forward.

The lady with whom I worked on my summer job at the hospital was unable to conceive how someone with a disability would be able to get a college education. Was it because of what may not have occurred in her life? I don't know. Did she have negative thoughts about herself that guided her life? I don't know. Remember, you can become what you think.

Aesop was a slave who lived in Greece more than two thousand years ago. He became famous for the fables he told to illustrate the wise and foolish behaviors of men. One of his stories was about a large oak tree. During a terrible storm a hurricane uprooted the oak tree and it was thrown across the way into a marshland. While the oak tree was lying there it looked around and said, "Here I lie, uprooted by the hurricane and thrown across the field. Yet you reeds, so thin and light, are still standing. How is that possible?" The reeds looked at the oak tree and responded by saying, "You fought against the winds generated from the hurricane. You are too proud to bend a little, so in the end you were destroyed. But we bowed before the winds, and so we still stand. We learned a long time ago that it's far better to bend than to break."

On the outside the oak tree appeared strong and mighty. It appeared able to withstand any trials and tribulations, troubles and obstacles. However, this was the appearance. Unfortunately, as the tree grew up over the years it became strong on the outside but never developed inward strength. How did this development affect the oak tree?

Often a person compensates for his/her insecurities by developing a strong outward appearance. Generally, a strong physique deters any challenges or negative attacks from others. However, the conscious decision to develop the outside to protect the inside can adversely affect you.

When challenged, some people respond with anger because they never developed a foundation to sustain them during difficult times. Unfortunately, they don't realize that the inner person needs developing. Otherwise every time a storm comes their foundation is shattered.

When a person develops a strong foundation, he/she learns to bend and not break, to give to the force without a compromise. They've learned how to respond to obstacles.

It's during these times that we can just bend and let the breeze pass us by, let the naysayers and negative talk pass us by, let the negative experience stretch us but not break us. Learning when to fight and when to just bend or bow is important to endure life's challenges. We must know when to stand and not fight back. Remember that your attitude can either make you or break you.

Do you have a challenge disguised as "I can't," "It's impossible," or "I don't have the time?" Desire it, require it, and obtain the freedom to accept the challenge. Unlock the shackles of self-imposed limitations and soar like an eagle. Believe in yourself.

P.S. Don't allow others to short-circuit your success. Remember to say and believe in your heart, "I can do it, I can do it. Yes I can, I know I can!"

Chapter 4

Accept a challenge as an opportunity to tap into the inner world of creativity. It's then that you will succeed.

CHAPTER 4

Power of the Mind

Creative Alternatives
The Laundromat

*H*ot Springs is a small town nestled in the mountains of Arkansas that is known for its hot thermal waters, which can be experienced on Bathhouse Row. I moved there in October when the beauty of the town can be seen as you drive through the mountains to get to the valley where the town rests.

Except for when I attended college, this was my first time living away from home. My job transferred me to Hot Springs when I was in my second year as an accountant trainee. I went there a few months prior and found an apartment in a nice neighborhood. My mom, oldest brother, sister, and the dog moved me to Hot Springs. I was excited but also apprehensive.

I didn't know anyone and no one knew me. While I was driving I wondered if I'd meet new friends. Would I find a church home? Would the people on the job be nice to me? So many questions ran through my mind. Regardless of the questions and a small level of anxiety, I knew this move would set me on a new path of self-discovery and awareness.

I had a lovely apartment in Hot Springs. It was located on the first floor and set up on a hill surrounded by beautiful trees. The first time I had to wash my clothes was difficult. It was easy to load the washer; however, I couldn't get all the clothes out of the washer. I stood there looking down into the washing machine wondering what to do.

When I was at home my mom or brother would unload the washer. I could reach the clothes closest to the top and middle, but I couldn't reach those at the bottom.

The first few times I washed I asked someone to pull the clothes out of the washer for me. However, that couldn't be the long-term solution because one time I waited almost thirty minutes for someone to come to the laundromat.

How was I going to get the clothes out of the washer? I tried using a clothes hanger, but it still required me to lean over into the tub (my head was in the tub) to pull the clothes out. Also, the hanger has a unique shape that made it difficult to pull the clothes out of the machine. The end of the hanger would get stuck while pulling the clothes to the top. Obviously, this wasn't going to work. I was becoming discouraged because I didn't like waiting for someone to help me. I wasn't free to wash when I wanted to.

One day I was cooking and needed to turn over my meat. I poked the fork in my meat and then turned it over to finish cooking. At that moment I realized how I was going to get the clothes out of the washer. Why didn't I think of this before? The same fork I was using to cook with could also be used to grab the clothes out of the washing machine.

The fork was at least twelve inches long, and the two prongs on the end were bent slightly so it could be used to lift something. What a marvelous idea to use the fork to pull my clothes out of the washer! I must be careful so that I didn't tear the clothes, but this could work.

After cooking I washed the fork and set it aside for its new assignment. The manufacturers made the fork for cooking, but I just gave it a new purpose. The next time I went to the laundromat I took with me the clothes, detergent, and my cooking fork. I was excited! As soon as the washer stopped I was able to pull the clothes out of the washer without having to wait for someone. At that point I began to realize the power of creativity.

What is the definition of creativity? Edward de Bono incorporates three diverse concepts into his definition of creativity. He states, "At the simplest level, [creativity] means bringing into being something which was not there before." Then he adds, "The new thing must have value," and lastly, it must include the concepts of "unexpectedness and change."

Initially I wasn't able to pull all of my clothes out of the washer. However, I never gave up. I needed to resolve my challenge. I wanted to conduct this activity by myself and on my own time. I kept thinking about how my fork was going to add value. I was excited about the opportunity to define a new use for the fork and experience the freedom I needed to wash when I wanted.

Eventually I was able to move from *can't* to *can*. My ability to pull my clothes out of the washer wasn't a new concept, but it heightened my ability to accept change and gave value to me.

The power of creativity compels you to be optimistic. It requires you to open your mind and be receptive to learn and discover new ways to resolve problems or, as I prefer to call it, "solve challenges."

God is the Master Creator of heaven and earth. All things were made by Him. Thus, who better to call on when we have a "how" question? God, how do I...? It's amazing how He has responded and shown me so many ways to accomplish the things I need to do.

The ability to solve a problem requires us to remain hopeful, confident, and steadfast. That's why we must ensure that we mentally place or keep ourselves on a path of self-discovery and awareness, because this too is the time when you can build your confidence. This is the time when you begin to see the possibilities in yourself.

As stated earlier, we must have the right attitude—an attitude open to receive new information, new ideas, and new ways of thinking and doing. I could have chosen to depend on others because we're supposed to help each other. However, God empowers us to function independent of others. God allows us the opportunity for freedom and privacy. When we doubt, all we need to do is ask and the Master will answer.

Other Discoveries

The automated teller machine (ATM) was one of the greatest technology changes of the twentieth century. The flexibility it provides to access your account at any time to withdraw or deposit money as well as review your account balances is phenomenal. The ATM removed the stress of trying to get to the bank before it closed.

The design of the ATM took into account many requirements for people with disabilities. Some of the keypads are large and readable for people visually impaired. Many of the machines have Braille. And for everyone the menu screens are intelligent and easy to walk through to access your account.

The debit card is the tool that is used to access your account via the ATM. Many ATMs require the cardholder to insert and withdraw the card to access the account. The card is held primarily by the thumb and first finger and then slid in and out of the card reader. The remaining steps to access your account are easy after that point.

When I needed to access my account, I had to ask someone to come with me because I couldn't insert the debit card in the reader. I knew there had to be a way for me to access my account without inconveniencing others. One evening I was shaping my eyebrows with a pair of tweezers. I was plucking one hair at a time. Standing there looking in the mirror I had a great idea. I could use the tweezers to grip my debit card and then slide it in and out of the card reader. I'll hold the tweezers with both arms and pick up the card by squeezing the tips together. Then I can push the card in the reader, and pull it back out. Well, I had to try out my new idea. I put a pair of tweezers in my wallet so I would have it for my next trip to the ATM.

Even though I didn't need any money, I had to go to the ATM to try my new idea. I pulled out my debit card and the tweezers. I gripped the card and successfully pulled it in and out of the reader. *Voila!* I did it. I eventually went to the store and purchased a pair of tweezers just for my purse. I was simply amazed.

God wants to help us use the creative part of our brain. Tapping into our creativity helps boost our confidence because we begin to learn new and exciting things. When I had a flat tire in Arkansas, I initially doubted myself without trying. I declared that I couldn't be successful and hadn't even tried. I looked at the fact that I didn't have hands and couldn't determine where I would get the strength needed to get the flat tire off. I had to open my mind to receive new information, a new way of changing a flat tire. If I hadn't allowed myself to move into a creative thinking mode, I would have missed the opportunity to build my confidence and hold fast to a "can do" spirit.

Don't limit your abilities because you'll squash your creativity, your fervor, your drive, and your desire. It's important to discipline yourself to keep trying. Don't give up. John C. Maxwell stated, "You will never find out what you can do until you do all you can to find out."

When I attended Northwestern State University in Natchitoches, Louisiana, I had to take a business machines class. The primary purpose of the class was to learn how to use an adding machine. This was a mandatory class to get a degree in accounting; thus, I couldn't avoid taking the class. I asked myself, "How are you going to pass this class without hands?"

Each finger and thumb is assigned to a set of numbers and function keys. The pinky finger was the most powerful because it controlled the primary function keys to add, subtract, multiply, and divide. The part that made me anxious initially was the fact that every test consisted of a set of math problems that had to be completed within an established timeframe by using the adding machine.

My first reaction after a few weeks was to drop the class and get a waiver from the dean, hoping to substitute it for a different class. However, I just couldn't do it. Dropping the class meant that I was giving up, throwing in the towel, admitting defeat. I decided I had to take the class.

Although I would attend class, I had to teach myself how to use the machine. I had to change my mindset and see the class as an opportunity to persevere, an opportunity to choose to win and not fail.

One of the things I learned was how to properly position the adding machine and my work papers to maximize my peripheral vision. Well, four months later after several practices and a test, I passed the class with a B.

Often it's difficult for people to have a "can do" spirit because they consider themselves unsuccessful before they even try. Sometimes we lack the confidence to see beyond where we are physically or mentally in our lives. We're afraid to think that we're worthy of success or that we're worthy of accomplishing a task presented to us or imposed by others. Eventually, we choose to give up without trying. We must choose to be a winner; we must choose to try and succeed. I could have chosen to depend on others to wash my clothes, but why when all it required me to do was rethink or reassess how I could pull the clothes out of the washing machine.

We must tap into the creative part of our brain. It's not acceptable to get to a block in the road and go back to start. Instead of moving in reverse, pause and create other options. Put on your thinking cap and draw on that creative part of the mind. Overcome the urge to give up.

Sometimes when I'm by myself I talk out loud to allow my speech pattern to overlay what I'm thinking. This ensures that my negative thinking surrenders to my heart and what I know about myself. I'm a survivor and more than a conqueror.

Seek the Master of all creation to help in time of need. We must take the time required to assess our situations and determine the correct approach or action. Sometimes ideas will come to you in minutes and at other times in days; however, do not give up. Always seek to know how to proceed.

Proverbs 30:26 states, "The rock badgers are a feeble folk, yet they make their homes in the crags." A rock badger is a very odd creature because it's said to have a mixture of other animal features, such as the incisors of a rodent and elephant's feet. However, it's a very slow-moving creature.

Although rock badgers move slowly, they have some interesting abilities. Rock badgers can look directly into the sun without distorting or damaging their vision. They have keen eyesight and can spot movement a mile away. The ability to see a mile away helps them to compensate for their slow movements. When a rock badger sees a predator approaching, it will have enough time to hide. Can you imagine being able to see a mile away?

It's interesting that the Bible selects this creature to demonstrate how we have what we really need to succeed. Isn't that amazing? The badger doesn't hide out in its home all day afraid to leave because of its physical limitations. No, it leaves its home and goes out to eat and lay out in the sun without worrying. He relies on what he can do as opposed to what he can't.

Perseverance is the ability to strive onward in times of hardship no matter what the obstacles may be. The rock badger's daily goal is to persevere. He remains persistent, diligent, and doesn't give up. This is the spirit we must have.

Say to yourself, "Despite what I don't have, I'll focus on what I do have and use it to prosper and live a successful and fulfilling life. I'll focus on what's good. I'll cherish the present and learn how to leave my crag and bask in the sun."

It Can Be Hard, but Press On

Your challenges may not be constrained by a physical or mental disability. You may be hindered because of the absence of perseverance, the absence of striving onward no matter what the obstacles may be. People give up on their goals and dreams because they don't want to take the time to rethink their approach or develop alternatives when faced with obstacles.

Sometimes you must step back and reassess how to attain your goal. When you don't see immediate results you must keep trying. Of course, let's not forget that we can become discouraged by others, but we must strive onward. We must press our way. Perseverance is a must have for success. It's the ability to strive onward in times of hardship no matter what the obstacles may be.

Our perseverance effort is driven by our dedication. I've learned that we're more determined to accomplish a task or goal when we have a passion for it. When you have a passion, it's not as difficult to excel. However, there are times when we must excel because we don't have a choice.

What is your passion? What is it that you desire to do? Is your passion or desire on hold because you won't persevere? I remember when I enrolled in graduate school. I took one course, and at the end of that semester I strongly considered not going back. I talked to family and friends, trying to find a champion who would agree with me. I couldn't imagine how or where I was going to muster the energy and stamina needed to get a graduate degree. The level of effort required and the numerous assignments were overwhelming.

School was difficult because I was working ten-hour days. My weekends soon became consumed with completing my homework assignments or meeting with my classmates to complete a research project. Although I made an A in my class the first semester, I thought that going back to school was not a good idea. Was I insane?

Over the Christmas holiday, I tried to convince myself that my dream of earning a graduate degree was old and stale. Earning a master's degree wasn't going to increase my salary, so what was the point? However, I remembered when I appeared on the *Ethel Odom* show at home in Alexandria, Louisiana, when I was a senior in high school. Ms. Odom asked me what I was going to do when I graduated from high school. I stated that I was going to go to college and earn a master's degree in business administration.

Well, I went to school but I stopped after I earned my bachelor's degree. Now after all these years, the opportunity finally presented itself. I didn't have a choice. Giving up was a major violation of my principle to have a "can do" spirit.

I converted to a coaching and mentoring role and began to self-talk. I had to make several adjustments because part of my difficulty with going back to school was the effect it had on my time after work. I was accustomed to going home after work and eating and relaxing.

Many times I watched television. I always watched *Wheel of Fortune* at seven o'clock, *Jeopardy* at seven-thirty, and then the regular line up for that day of the week. My mindset at the time was that school was interfering with my weeknight shows, such as *CSI, 24, Law and Order,* and movies on HBO or Showtime.

Coupled with not wanting to put in the extra effort to study and complete the assignments, I decided that "I didn't have the time." That's when I had to step back and reassess my goals and determine my priorities. Although watching television is a great pastime, it wasn't going to help me accomplish my goals. Spending my time watching television was not going to help me fulfill my purpose in life.

I soon learned that going back to school was the best decision I could have ever made. Each semester my coursework was research or information that I could use on my job. Often I attended a meeting the next day on a topic we had just covered in class. It was an awesome experience. The more classes I took, the more I realized that the timing was great.

I had always vowed that if I ever went back to school I would do better than I did during undergraduate. Well, I graduated with a 4.0 grade point average and earned a Master of Science degree in accounting.

People have asked me, "How did you do it? How did you work long hours and go to school? How did you take care of your home?" My response to them: "Amazing grace." Grace simply means the favor of God. One of the verses to the song "Amazing Grace" says, "The Lord has promised good to me, His word my hope secures; He will my shield and portion be, as long as life endures."

It can be hard at times to keep going once you get started because we must adjust our schedules and become better time managers. Generally, time management is our biggest challenge. Time management requires us to assess our daily activities and determine better ways to accomplish our tasks, including the elimination of non-value-added activities. Overall, watching television for numerous hours is a non-value-added activity. We must be diligent, which is the persistent effort to accomplish a task or goal. The Bible states, "The hand of the diligent will rule" (Proverbs 12:24a). We all must learn to continuously press forward, to persevere, to be diligent when obstacles are in our way. However, we must ensure that we recognize our obstacles so that we can make the appropriate adjustments.

People tell me they want to go back to school but say they can't because they have children, thus declaring that their children are obstacles. Well, I say to them that the children aren't the obstacle but inadequate time management is. We're empowered to make decisions that will benefit the entire family and then assess and adjust.

Assess and Adjust

One day I was leaving my apartment in Hot Springs to go to work. As I walked toward my car I noticed it was leaning to the side. Upon careful inspection I wanted to scream, "Oh no, I have a flat tire! What am I going to do? Who's going to change the tire? I must get to work." I ran back into the apartment and began to cry. Why was this happening to me? I didn't know anyone; I'd only been there a few months.

I continued to cry and wondered why I accepted the position to move five hours from home. "Lord, You need to help me," I prayed. "I don't know what to do." As I continued to call out to God visions of changing a tire came to me showing me step by step what to do. I began to feel better. I stood and told myself, *Karren, you can change that tire.*

I changed clothes and went outside. I took the jack out of the trunk, loosened the bolts, and jacked up the car. So far, so good. I removed the flat tire and put on the spare, put the bolts back on, and began to lower the car. As I watched the car lower to the ground, the strangest thing began to happen. The spare tire looked low. When I finally lowered the car, the spare tire was not just low; it too was flat. No, this couldn't be happening to me—another flat tire.

While I was inspecting the flat tire, three people passed by me going to the trash bin, two men and a lady. I just knew that one of the guys would assist me, but one of them quickened his pace and went back into his apartment. The lady smiled and spoke and went to her apartment as well. They didn't offer to help.

My goodness, what am I supposed to do? I thought. Well, I looked in the trunk of the car and remembered that the "donut" (the manufacturer spare) was in the trunk. So I jacked the car up again, removed the second flat tire, and put the donut on. This time I said a prayer: "Please, Lord, please don't let this tire be flat." I lowered the car, and *ta-da* the spare was good. I was so excited. I did it. I changed the flat tire. Wow, I was so amazed.

You'll never know or understand why you face challenges in your life. But despite those challenges you must be persistent and diligent to endure life's journey. You must refuse to give up.

I ran back into my apartment, changed clothes, and headed for work. When I got to work, I told my supervisor and co-workers what had happened. They were amazed. The more I told the story, the better I felt; my spirits were lifted.

After work I went to the store to have both tires fixed. The attendant asked, "Who changed your tire?" I looked at him with the biggest smile and said, "I did." He said, "No you didn't." I said, "Yes I did." He said, "No way. That's amazing. How could you do that?"

It was then that I realized why I was so excited that morning, why I had such a spirit of expectation that morning when I woke up. Somehow I knew something good was going to happen, but I didn't know what. Now I knew.

God's Word says, "In quietness and confidence shall be your strength" (Isaiah 30:5). I was so lonely, missing my mom and siblings. I had even begun to miss the dog. I realized that I was afraid of what would happen. What if I couldn't do certain things for myself? What would I do? Who would be there to help?

That morning God spoke to me and reminded me that He was my help. The same hand that had guided me thus far was still there for me. He reminded me to continue to look to Him for guidance and assistance. What a day, what a day, what a day.

That tire-changing event significantly boosted my confidence and self-esteem. I was happy about how I was encouraging myself. Many people look for others to encourage them, but there are times when we must encourage ourselves.

Getting beyond obstacles is like being in a boat paddling upstream. It's hard and sometimes seems outright impossible, but you must keep paddling to get to the top of the stream. Be determined to press onward.

P.S. Remember, it's better to accept a challenge as an opportunity to tap into the inner world of creativity. It's then that you will succeed. Perseverance is fundamental to your success. Learn how to assess and adjust so that you can strive onward in times of hardship, no matter what the obstacles may be. Be persistent, be diligent, and endure life's journey.

Chapter 5

*I'm only one, but I'm one, I cannot do everything,
but I can do something, and that which I can do,
by the grace of God I will do.*

Dwight L. Moody

CHAPTER 5

Courage

Hold on to the Left or Take the Right?

*C*an you be totally successful and lack courage as well as confidence? I don't think you can. Courage coupled with confidence is the state of mind that enables one to face situations without threat or fear. It's the state of mind to have faith and believe in yourself.

What is total success? I define it as the favorable outcome of your goals and dreams with a fullness of joy. Many people are successful but don't have joy in their lives or else very little.

Total success is relative and is measured differently depending on what you're trying to accomplish. Oftentimes total success is hampered, delayed, or we don't achieve our goals and dreams because we're not willing to let go of the past. The past can represent offenses from others or mistakes that we've made. Can you let go of the past?

Someone asked me one day if I was upset about not having hands. I thought about the question and took a quick trip down memory lane. Years ago when I first moved to Arkansas I did wonder if my life would be different if I had hands. I wondered if people would respond to me differently, treat me kinder. I began to assess how my life would be different. I asked myself, "Is there anything you want to do that you haven't been able to do?" But the main question I asked myself was, "Can you turn back the hands of time?" Well, the answer to that question is no.

I can't go back in time and reverse the past. So then what's the point of answering the first question, "Is there anything you want to do that you haven't been able to do?" I said, "Well, I've done and will continue to do not only those things that I need to do but what I want to do as well."

You must be willing to set aside past experiences, offenses, and mistakes. Your goals should be so big that you don't have time to dwell on what happened. You only have time to focus on the present and future.

Everyone has to make a break with the past. If you've been offended by others you must forgive them and move on. You could have also made poor decisions. These decisions may have hurt others or yourself. In this situation forgive yourself. It's important to let go of old emotions and realize that the past is over and done. Again, you cannot change the past; you cannot turn back the hands of time because the past has passed.

Imagine that you're standing with your hands stretched out to your sides parallel with your shoulders. The event named Future is holding your right hand and the event named Past is holding your left hand. Neither Future nor Past has successfully pulled you in their direction.

Future is telling you there's excitement and great adventures ahead. Future tells you there will be times when you're challenged and must make tough decisions, but it attempts to assure you that this is the right path to take; life is easier going forward than backwards.

Past is holding your left hand attempting to convince you that you can only be and do what you have experienced.

You've experienced not being successful or completing a task, and thus you'll never be successful. Past tells you that your feelings of disappointment and emotions of despair are okay. Past tells you to remember all of your experiences, to take a walk down memory lane and recount your failures. Past tells you that recalling your failures will serve as evidence that your future will be the same.

Future hears Past telling you to walk down memory lane and agrees, but Future suggests that you recall your successes and victories. Future says to recall your successes regardless of the number or the type. Future says to look at your failures as well and ask yourself while in that situation did you ever think you were going to make it.

Future says to count what looked like a failure as a success because you didn't perish. Count these past events as victories. Future tells you that recounting the past in a negative way can render you powerless. It reminds you that the past can either build you up or tear you down. Future reminds you to cherish the past but to get excited about the future.

Future is holding your right hand, asking you to believe in yourself and do what is right. Since this is God's declaration to us, we must go right to the Future. It's no coincidence that Past is holding your left hand. The left hand represents the past.

Because Past is holding your left hand, it's an indication of a place, person, or thing that You must go away from or depart. The right thing to do is to move into the Future. The Future represents God for He says in His word, "For I the Lord thy God will hold thy right hand, saying unto thee, Fear not; I will help thee" (Isaiah 41:13). Therefore, move to the future.

My parents taught us the Twenty-third Psalm at a young age. My favorite verse in this psalm is "thou anointest my head with oil" (Psalm 23:5b). For years I knew that the verse was powerful, but I never clearly understood why until I researched the Scripture to understand why the shepherd anointed the sheep's head. The shepherd is responsible for protecting his flock. Because the flock grazed in the field, the shepherd would rub the oil on their heads, especially around the nostrils. The nose bats would swarm around the sheep but never bother them because of the oil.

A nose bat is a mature fly, dark gray, and about the size of a bee. These pests are found primarily in the frontal sinuses of sheep. When the larvae are deposited by the fly on the edge of the nostril, the grubs are less than one-twelfth of an inch in size. They cause an irritation as they crawl through the nostrils and gradually move up the nasal passages. The resulting inflammation causes a thin secretion that becomes quite thick if infection occurs, making it difficult for the sheep to breathe, and it may sneeze frequently.

The sheep may become run-down because of their lack of appetite. They're also stressed because they can't graze in peace. Sheep put their heads to the ground, stamp, and suddenly run with their heads down to avoid this fly. They often become frantic and press their noses in the ground or against other sheep as the flies attack them, which is usually during the heat of the day.

When I worked in Arkansas, my office was right by the main door to our office. Every morning I watched the people from the other staffs pass back and forth as they all made their way to the coffee room. The coffee room offered an opportunity in the morning for people to share about their evening or make plans for lunch. It was a great opportunity to socialize.

Every morning a guy who worked in the engineering department would stop by and speak. He was a nice guy. He would stop and say, "Good morning, young-un." And I returned the welcome by saying, "Good morning." He always walked around with a cup of coffee and a toothpick in his mouth. One morning he stopped by our office and leaned against the doorframe. He sucked his teeth, and while shifting the toothpick in his mouth he said, "I don't know why you were hired. You can't write, type, or use a calculator, and you're supposed to be an accountant."

I sat there feeling as if I had just been struck by an eighteen-wheeler. I was devastated! What could I say? After he made the statement he walked on to the coffee room to get a cup of coffee. I was in shock, a state of disbelief. No one had ever told me that I was unqualified to perform my duties.

After that day I was suspicious of the entire office especially the folks on my floor. There were a few people who would huddle together. For some unknown reason I always thought they were talking about me.

Weeks and months went by. I couldn't set aside the fact that this man basically stated that I shouldn't have been hired. I was sad and began to imagine that the entire town was watching me. Every day I would go home and not go out until the next day.

I didn't like the way I felt. I always felt sad and miserable. I decided one evening that I had to correct his assessment. One morning I stopped him when he was on his way to the coffee room. I said, "Hey, I want to show you something." He stepped into my office while I pulled out a sheet of paper. I took the paper and signed my name. Then I put a piece of paper in the typewriter and typed a few words. The engineer stood with his mouth wide open in awe. Then I turned on the calculator and added some numbers. Needless to say, word of the demonstration spread throughout the office. I was giving more and more demonstrations.

Has anyone ever dampened your confidence by disputing your capabilities or actions? If so, this person is a discourager disguised as a human nose bat. This person tells you things that irritate you and leave you feeling stressed and depressed. You toss and turn in your bed at night because you can't sleep. You attempt to modify your action plans to accomplish your goals, and now you can't think clearly. You're confused and just want to sleep through the days and nights hoping that a miraculous change will come.

You replay their comments over and over in your mind. The discourager's motive may not have been impure, but the comment still hurts. For example, you've shared that you want to open a restaurant. Their comment may be, "Well, I don't think people are interested in another restaurant." They're basically stating that you're not going to be successful. If they were really interested in your business venture they could have asked, "How can I help?" Instead of asking questions, they indirectly decide that you're going to fail.

You can ensure that you're not stopped in your tracks on your journey by believing in your heart, soul, and mind that you're anointed. Ensure that you have the Word in your heart to recite in times of trouble. The Word of God is the most effective mechanism to defeat comments that come along to distract, discourage, or make you frantic so that you don't trust your path or direction.

I lived in Hot Springs for about four years and then was selected for a position in Asheville, North Carolina. Moving from the flatlands in Louisiana to the inclines in Arkansas to the mountains in North Carolina was exhilarating. I was so excited because I was getting a promotion and moving up in my federal career.

Many people couldn't understand why I accepted a job on the East Coast or, as they said, "Way over there." However, I knew that Arkansas wasn't my final destination. Before I left, some friends were telling me to just wait and find another job closer to Hot Springs so that I could remain close to Louisiana. But it was difficult to describe to people that my spirit said it was time to go. I had become antsy and restless. There was something stirring up in me preparing me for the next move, and I wasn't afraid.

Move on or Stay?

I received my travel authorization, arranged for the transfer of my household goods, and down the road I went. I was going to a place I had never been before, to do what I had never done before. However, I reminded myself that my life is a journey. I reminded myself that my lifelong mission is to seek out new places and new opportunities and to boldly go and do what I had never done before. Boy, was I excited.

I remember driving down the highway getting bored. After miles of highway driving I had seen enough houses, fields, and cows. The drive was boring. At one point I started to wonder if I had made the right decision. I was going to a place where I had never lived and didn't know anyone. I was going to work on a job supervising a staff for the first time.

Would I be a good supervisor or bad? Had I learned enough to be successful? Were people going to like me? How would people react to my style of operating? Was I the best qualified? At one point I asked myself, "Have you lost your mind?"

Suddenly I had mixed emotions. I was sad yet glad, but my sadness was beginning to overshadow me. Just when doubt began to creep into my mind I decided to encourage and motivate myself. Since I like music, I decided to make up songs. One song I started to sing was to the tune of "This Old Man." The more I sang the song, the better I felt and the more miles I drove. Boy, did I feel good.

I smiled at people as I drove down the highway, waving and grinning. The words to the song were, "I love me, yes I do, I'm as happy as can be, with a great big hug and a kiss from me to me, this ol' girl is feeling free." I felt free. The freedom I was experiencing was the escape from doubt, the escape from fear, the escape from anxiety. I embraced courage and knew that the God I served who kept me in Hot

Springs would keep me in Asheville. I had to move on to my next assignment.

Don't create an atmosphere of fear and doubt to complicate your journey. Someone told me that fear is false evidence appearing real or incorrect facts that appear to be true. That's why the Bible tells us to cast down imaginations. I was feeling really good because my move represented courage and faith. I was moving to yet another town where I didn't know anyone.

What is your next move? It may not be to another city, but is it in the form of the next steps that must be taken to fulfill your purpose in life? What are you going to do? Well, I'll help you by saying, "Move on." It's time to get going.

Remember, you're the driver. You must have courage. Courage isn't always loud and boastful. In some cases courage is the quiet, gentle hand and Word of God extended to you saying, "There is tomorrow." That voice won't scold and rebuke but rather encourage you to have faith and believe in yourself.

P.S. Remember, you cannot do all things but do everything related to fulfilling your purpose in life.

Chapter 6

Become a voyager open to explore, to learn and live a fulfilling life.

CHAPTER 6

The Journey Begins

*A*lthough we can't change the past we do have the power to direct our future. Go back into your hall of memory and find the courage to view those experiences. Only this time view your history through the clear vision of retrospection. Give yourself the answers you didn't have then and learn what you once failed to learn. Then let it go. When you do this you will be free.

There's a story of a bird that lives deep in the snowy mountains. Tortured by night's numbing cold, it cries to build a warm nest in the morning. Yet, when day breaks, it sleeps the day away basking in the warmth of the sun. So it continues crying vainly throughout its life.

Many people are like this bird. They'd rather moan about their situation than make a change. They let opportunity after opportunity pass them by because they don't want to put forth the effort to change. If you've taken the time to read this book, I expect that you have now decided you're not like that bird.

Mr. Young, my dad, knew his assignment was to ensure that I understood that the use of the word *can't* would impose and establish limitations. Using the word *can't* establishes boundaries and lowers expectations. He knew that *can't* is a disempowering word.

We must exemplify our values and establish a foundation supported by perseverance, courage, commitment, and faith. These foundational truths are supported by a high measure of endurance, dedication, commitment, and conviction. All of these are driven by passion, which is an intense emotional drive for something we love.

Changing our inward convictions leads to results. You must desire a positive attitude, a can-do spirit, by changing your inward conviction. Think and say "I can." Think and say "I'm able." Think and say "I will." Then after all the thinking and saying, do it!

What is it that you were born for? What is it that motivates you, stirs you whenever the topic is mentioned? What is that? That's whatever motivates you. A burning desire arises whenever "that" is mentioned or talked about. Think about it. What is it? Whatever it is, you were born for it.

Prepare to train for it, and be ready to use it to fulfill your purpose, to accomplish your goals and objectives. What are people capable of doing? No one knows. You don't know what you're capable of doing. When I registered for driver's education in high school, no one knew how I was going to drive. However, I decided that I wanted to drive. We must not restrain our thoughts and actions.

Real victory has to do with the mindset. Be happy with yourself. Access your will for joy. Joy is prosperous and strengthening. Joy helps to eliminate self-imposed limitations. We must unlock the shackles and experience freedom.

When I was in grade school, I loved to play dodge ball. The object of the game is to eliminate all opposing players by making contact with a thrown ball; thus, there's a ball and several people on the field. The ball is thrown, and if it makes contact with you, you're out of the game. Whoever gets the ball has the opportunity to throw it. You must keep moving and dodge the ball when it's thrown at you. Generally, the one who is fast, watchful, and alert wins the game. The will to survive is intense.

The need to move quickly and avoid getting hit by the ball when it's tossed your way is a must. There are times when you're successful, and then there are times when you get hit and must wait until the game begins again. So what do you do when hit? Study the game, learn the moves, apply lessons learned. Sometimes you must SLEEP on it. That is, you need to Study, Learn, Endure, and be Encouraged to Press your way.

Don't give up but give more. Press your way to success. Don't deprive yourself of the liberties you deserve. Don't deprive yourself of being a winner, a champion, and the last one standing.

One of the components that form the basis of our attitude is information. Information is made available to us when we are growing up based on our experiences or the experiences of others. Throughout the years, we categorize information in our minds and recall it to make decisions, form opinions, and trigger our emotional reactions.

When new information is presented to us, we recall in our minds what we may know about the information and either make a decision or form an opinion. Oftentimes we make what we learn agree with what we already know. For example, when anyone who doesn't know me sees me, he/she immediately thinks that because I don't have hands, I can't write, eat, or drive.

They make this decision because the information stored in their mind, based on their experience, indicates that you must have hands to hold a fork or write. The same is true with driving. Your information base searches the driving category of your mind and tells you that a person must have hands to drive or else their car must be equipped with special devices. Therefore, when a person sees me, he/she immediately determines that I can't write, eat, or drive.

I've lived in several states, and getting a driver's license is always an interesting experience. One of the states I lived in refused to give me a license. They stated that I had to take driving lessons and install a special device in my car before they would issue me a license. I told the people to come and look at my car and let me take the driving test there at the office to prove I could drive, but they said no.

I appealed the decision, and about a month later I received a letter in the mail scheduling a road test. A man from the motor vehicle department came to observe and document the test. He first examined my car and jotted down a few notes. I got in the car and drove about half a mile when he said, "I've seen enough. You can go back to your home."

What took over a month to accomplish was over in less than a minute. I was new information to the people at the motor vehicle department, but they refused to give me an opportunity to enhance their knowledge base. They'd rather make me fit into the category of information they thought they knew about all drivers, which is that you must have hands or special devices to drive.

You must ensure that you're open to new information. Don't always make assumptions based on what you know. I remember when my husband and I were buying groceries and I pulled out the checkbook to write a check. The cashier looked at my husband and stated bluntly, "You should be writing the check. Why are you making her do that? She can't write." Well, my husband ignored her and continued to read the magazine.

I looked at her and wrote the check. When I finished writing the check, she looked at me, looked at the check, and screamed, "Oh, my God! You all need to see this. She can write!" Although I was a little embarrassed, I had the opportunity to update her knowledge component. In the future she should no longer look at someone and assume they can't. Now she can assume they can.

Be careful! Don't allow a person's reaction based on their information to influence your emotions. This is important so that we don't let the emotional component of our attitude influence the action component of our attitude. We must learn to control our response to people's comments or reactions so that we don't in turn offend others.

I was offended when people would say to me, "I feel sorry for you." One time someone suggested that I should wear long sleeves all the time to hide my arms. I had a decision to make based on their reaction: get upset or just be MAD and ignore the comment. I decided to always brush off these types of comments and allow them to be an opportunity for someone to know that God's grace is sufficient for me.

How do you react when you're presented with new information, whether it's people, places, or things? What emotion is triggered? Is the emotion positive or negative? Is it full of joy or anger? How do you react when you are new information to other people?

My hands were amputated to save my life. The doctors couldn't save my hands and if they waited any longer they wouldn't be able to save me. A cutting had to take place, a separation from that part of me that had died in order that I may live. Unbeknownst to a lot of people, that day established a new beginning in my life. Yes, I was only three, but even at that age my destiny and purpose in life was being shaped and developed. The stage for my message was being developed.

The foundation was established that I might be the vessel to set people free, that I might be a visual reminder for people that all things are possible if you believe. No one can determine your abilities.

What should you figuratively cut off to save your life? What should be removed from your life to improve the quality of your living? Whose comments do you need to ignore because the words are like nose bats, hindering you from stepping out and fulfilling your dreams?

Take a sheet of paper and draw a full-body picture of yourself holding a bag. The contents of the bag contain all the negative things that people have said about you or what you've said about yourself. The contents represent a series of mistakes you've made or inappropriate decisions you've made.

Now get a pair of scissors and cut the bag out of the picture. This action represents a separation from the past, from what has held you back, from what has kept you sitting on your dreams and prevented you from fulfilling your purpose in life.

Draw a new bag right by your feet. This bag contains the attributes of the new you: self-acceptance, self-love, confidence, boldness, courage, perseverance, motivation, determination. The bag is at your feet available to you whenever you need a reminder of who you are and the power that resides inside. You don't need to carry the bag around because it's in you.

These attributes are not there to weigh you down but to lift you up. These attributes are the fuel to keep you motivated and encouraged for the rest of your life, to ensure that you're not just satisfied but living life to its fullest.

One of my favorite television shows when I was a child was *Star Trek*. I was intrigued with the storyline and impressed with the boldness of Captain Kirk and his crew. Each adventure was surprising and adventurous. You always knew that the captain was going to romance someone on the show; however, you never knew where they would go, what they would see, or the obstacles and challenges they would encounter. This was definitely a mysterious show.

Every week I was glued to the television. I had memorized the opening statement and followed how that statement exemplified the crew's experience. As soon as I heard the music I knew it was time for my show. The starship would appear flying through the galaxy, and then the music would begin. A voice would say, "We are the voyagers of the starship Enterprise. Our five-year mission is to explore strange new worlds, to seek out new lives and new civilizations, and to boldly go where no man has gone before." I loved it. For one hour I watched as the story unfolded showing their challenges, adventures, places, people, and even things. So over the years I developed my own statement flowing with the same rhythm. My mission statement reads, "I'm a voyager of the Christian enterprise. My lifelong mission is to explore strange new places, to seek out new opportunities and challenges, and to boldly go and do what I've never done before."

Ephesians 3:20-21 states that God can do exceedingly and abundantly above all that we ask or think according to the power that works in us. Note that the power is in *you* to boldly go and do what you've never done before.

There's a Japanese proverb that states, "The closer you stand to the lighthouse, the darker it is." Many people waste their time and energy trying to get rid of the darkness. Or they keep doing the same thing expecting different results, and what they find is that they're still in darkness. The key is to increase the light, and the light can only be increased by stepping out in faith and trusting God to help you do the things you've never done before.

I moved from Hot Springs, Arkansas, to Asheville, North Carolina, and then to New Orleans, and now I reside in Maryland. Often I reflect on that song I heard for the first time at the church conference in New Orleans. I can now embrace the song and sing it in its entirety. "Look at me, I'm a testimony, I didn't make it on my own. I'm not standing here alone. It was Jesus who gave me this opportunity. Look at me, I'm a testimony."

P.S. The only way to discover what is possible in your life is to go beyond what you're currently capable of doing. Go beyond the possible, embrace the impossible, and watch the impossible become possible. Let your trust and faith in God replace doubt and fear. Isaiah 41:13 states, "...the Lord your God will hold your right hand, saying to you, Fear not, I will help you."

About the Author

*K*arren Y. Alexander demonstrates on a daily basis that all things are possible if you believe. As a motivational and inspirational speaker, she encourages people to live beyond satisfaction and achieve the impossible by eliminating self-imposed limitations.

Karren has been a teacher, as well as a conference and keynote speaker, for corporations, organizations, and Christian audiences across the United States. Her goal is to encourage people to believe in their hearts that all things are possible. However, she believes that the heart can only be changed and sustained when the verbal speech pattern agrees. The change in verbal speech pattern begins by eliminating disempowering words such as "can't."

Karren is the founder of PAMD International, LLC. PAMD is an acronym describing her foundational principles and life-sustaining belief, which is to be *P*ositive with an *A*ttitude of *M*otivation and *D*etermination.

Karren was born and raised in Alexandria, Louisiana. She has a dual undergraduate degree in accounting and management and a Master of Science degree in accounting. She started her federal career twenty-five years ago and has worked in various budget and finance positions in the states of Louisiana, Arkansas, North Carolina, and the District of Columbia.

Karren and her husband, Michael, reside in Bowie, Maryland.

Bibliography

Maxwell, John C. *The Journey from Success to Significance* (Nashville, TN: J. Countryman, 2004), 27, 32.

McGovern, Ann (retold by). *Aesop's Fables* (New York: Scholastic, 1963), 75.

Meyer, Joyce. *Knowing God Intimately* (New York: Time Warner Book Group, 2003), 207.

Tanner, Tanner. *101 Reasons to Get up in the Morning: Celebrities' Favourite Inspirational Quotes* (UK: Canterbury Press, 2005), 90, 117.

The American College Dictionary (New York: Random House, 1968)

http://library.thinkquest.org/C0110299/mind/creativity. php?page=creativity0, January 2, 2007. The Brain Explorer, Creativity Home

http://njnj.essortment.com/rockbadger_rhwe.htm http, 2002, The Rock Badger, ads by Google.